New Entries

LEARNING BY WRITING AND DRAWING

★ ★ ★

EDITED BY

Ruth Shagoury Hubbard

AND

Karen Ernst

HEINEMANN

Portsmouth, NH

Heinemann

A division of Reed Elsevier Inc.

361 Hanover Street

Portsmouth, NH 03801-3912

Offices and agents throughout the world

The editors and publisher wish to thank those who have generously given permission to reprint borrowed material:

Portions of Chapter 10 originally appeared in an article by Jean Anne Clyde and Heidi Mills in *Dimensions of Early Childhood* (Winter 1993). Reprinted by permission of the editor.

Basketball cards on page 126 are reprinted by permission of NBA Properties, Inc. *Left:* © 1993 NBA Properties, Inc. *Right:* 1991 NBA Properties, Inc.

Library of Congress Cataloging-in-Publication Data

New entries : learning by writing and drawing / edited by Ruth
    Shagoury Hubbard and Karen Ernst.
        p.   cm.
    Includes bibliographical references.
    ISBN 0-435-07204-8 (alk. paper)
    1. Language arts.   2. English language—Composition and exercises—
Study and teaching.   3. Drawing.   4. Imagination.   5. Active learning.
    I. Hubbard, Ruth, 1950–   II. Ernst, Karen.
    LB1576.N427   1996
    372.6'23—dc20   96-4155
                                                                  CIP

Editor: Toby Gordon
Production: Vicki Kasabian
Book design: Joni Doherty
Cover design: Michael Leary
Manufacturing: Louise Richardson

Printed in the United States of America on acid-free paper

99 98 97 96   EB   1 2 3 4 5

Contents

Acknowledgments

Many people contributed to the success of this project. Our first thanks go to the contributors, who carved time out of their busy professional life to work on their chapter. From the beginning their enthusiasm and innovation inspired us, nudging us to take new risks in our own learning and teaching.

The idea for this collection grew from a spirited conversation with our editor and friend, Toby Gordon. Without her commitment to the project and her interest in broader definitions of literacy, this book would not exist. We thank her for her support, her keen insights, and her willingness to respond to our sometimes frantic phone calls with calming advice and good humor. Alan Huisman guided our prose with his green pencil; we're grateful for his detailed comments and careful copyediting.

Ruth wishes to thank the folks that kept her going throughout the process, especially Brenda Power, Jill Ostrow, Kimberly Campbell, Jody Rutherford, Nancy Winterbourne, Linda Christensen, Mary Burke-Hengen, Caryl Hurtig, Joan Becker, Teresa Patterson, and Brynna Hurwitz. Karen thanks Maureen Miletta, Kathleen Reilly, Angela Wormser-Reid, Peter von Euler, Lyn Gehr, Hallie Cirino, Mary Sue Welch, and Dawn Damiani for inviting her into their classrooms and showing how new ideas can take shape in many ways.

And always, a thousand thanks to our partners in life, Jim Whitney and Augusto daSilva. With their enthusiasm and willingness to listen to our drafts of thought, they encourage us to share our common languages with others, writing and drawing ideas about expanding literacy.

Introduction

Communication. Exploration. Expression. These terms are at the heart of literacy instruction. How do we create and share meaning? And how do we help our students deal effectively with their world in ways that are satisfying to themselves and their communities?

Teaching and learning in schools has tended to focus on words, written and spoken, as the building blocks for understanding the world and passing on knowledge to others. Drawing and image making have been separate from the regular curriculum, treated more often as decoration than as tools for exploring the world and ourselves. But when images and words work together to create meaning, literacy's potential expands.

Peter von Euler's drawing on the cover of this book is one of the new entries he is making in his journal and in his learning. Like too many of us, his education followed a route that dictated he put aside his crayons, paints, and drawing pencils in elementary school. But in the last few years, he has taken them up again in order to help his students use art in their classroom learning. Drawing in his own journal led him to understand the process from the inside out. He is embracing a wider range of possibilities in his teaching and in his notions of what literacy can be.

Donald Graves reminded his audience at the University of New Hampshire Literacy Conference (October 1995) that we are the best teachers when we are teaching on the edge of what we are currently learning. The authors in this collection are immersed in the twin composition crafts of writing and drawing. They are making new entries into their learning as teachers, exploring ways to incorporate the visual arts into literacy instruction and into their own life as well.

New Entries: Learning by Writing and Drawing is an invitation to take art beyond making pretty pictures and into exploring the world. Teachers from primary school through college bring you into their classroom and show how writing, art, and reading can be combined in different content areas.

You'll meet Jill Ostrow's classroom of mathematical thinkers who go "beyond answers" when they grapple with sophisticated number concepts; get an inside view of how Mary Stein and Brenda Power invite their students to "put art on the scientist's palette"; and learn with Peter Thacker as he explains his process of combining imagery and story in his high school reading class.

The powerful *practical theory* revealed in the story of Karen Ernst's artists workshop is extended in Nancy Winterbourne's second-grade literacy workshop. Irene Fountas and Jan Olson describe classroom learners moving back and forth between visual and verbal expression, each language informing the other.

We also take you in for a closer look with a couple of case studies of individual children. Our collection begins with Susan Benedict's insightful case study of Rachel. By sharing her own nature journal entries, Susan was able to "draw in" a reluctant reader and writer, building on Rachel's eye for detail, her observation skills, and her passion for the natural world. Jean Anne Clyde takes us deep into six-year-old Douglas's process of creating and extending his understanding.

Visual expression is a human capacity possessed by *everyone*. Our final chapters show that it's never too late to pick up our drawing tools and bring them into our learning environment. In order for teachers to infuse drawing into their curriculum, they have found they must take up where they left off in childhood in order to experience picture making for themselves.

And it isn't only in school experiences but also in the wider world that these tools can serve us well. Toby Gordon's concluding chapter "Drawing My Selves Together" takes a look at how it has changed her life to begin to write and draw in her notebooks as a way to test out ideas in her personal and professional world.

It has been our privilege as coeditors of this volume to work with a growing number of other educators who share our passion for writing and art. We hope these stories will intrigue you and make you eager to try out some of the strategies within these pages—and to branch out with innovations of your own.

1

Drawing Rachel In

Susan Benedict

I first met Rachel three years ago when I joined the faculty of the Center for Teaching and Learning. She was a pint-sized fourth grader whose light brown hair was almost long enough to sit on. Her peers introduced her to me as the Center's resident expert on—and supreme collector of—tiny stuffed hedgehogs. Although Rachel maintained a low profile in large groups, she occasionally spoke at our school's morning assemblies to encourage everyone to support the local animal shelter by donating supplies.

When she became one of my students the following year, I learned that Rachel's favorite parts of the school day were math, gym (when the activity was track and field), and artists workshop. She particularly liked activities that had a defined agenda or could be measured: in math she enjoyed manipulating numbers more than solving problems; in gym she strove to beat her personal best as a runner; and in art she loved to try to capture the natural world realistically with pencil and paint. Early on I also learned that Rachel and I would find it challenging to work together during two thirds of her school day—the parts that involved reading, writing, and social studies.

Rachel loved to be read to. Her parents took an active interest in her learning, and they valued reading. They read books with her and to her and recommended books they felt she might enjoy reading. They reported that Rachel frequently pored over reference books to identify birds or to find the answers to questions. But somehow, when she read longer texts on her own, the stories did not come alive for her in the way they did when a more experienced reader used his or her voice to bridge the gap between Rachel's understanding and her reading ability.

An informal reading inventory I administered revealed that Rachel could read with a minimal number of miscues. She readily retold "Shells" by Cynthia Rylant (1985) after reading the story to me aloud. Although she had some difficulty identifying a theme statement and offered minimal definition of the characters, her reading skills seemed adequate for a beginning fifth grader. But Rachel did not find reading easy; when she read, it was not for enjoyment but to find answers. Reading was a tool, not an end in itself. Rachel, her parents,

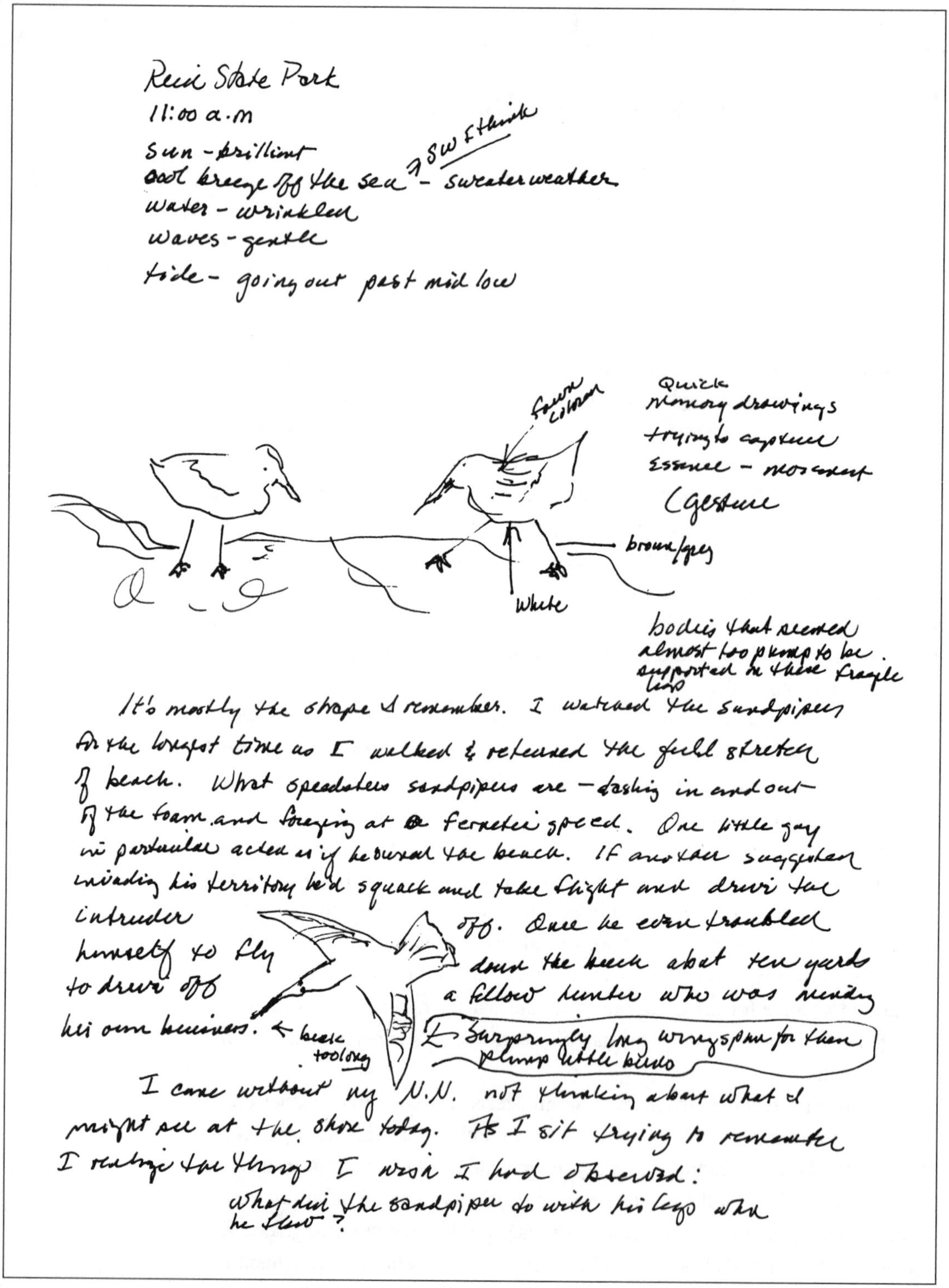

Reid State Park
11:00 a.m
Sun - brilliant
cool breeze off the sea ↗ SW I think - sweater weather
water - wrinkled
waves - gentle
tide - going out past mid low

color xxx

Quick
memory drawings
trying to capture
essence - movement
(gesture

brown/grey

white

bodies that seemed
almost too plump to be
supported on these fragile
legs

It's mostly the shape I remember. I watched the sandpipers
for the longest time as I walked & retraced the full stretch
of beach. What speedsters sandpipers are — dashing in and out
of the foam and foraging at a frenetic speed. One little guy
in particular acted as if he owned the beach. If another suggested
invading his territory he'd squawk and take flight and drove the
intruder   off. Once he even troubled
himself to fly   down the beach about ten yards
to drive off   a fellow hunter who was minding
his own business." ← beak   [↱ Surprisingly long wingspan for these
                     too long   plump little birds]

I came without my N.N. not thinking about what I
might see at the shore today. As I sit trying to remember
I realize the things I wish I had observed:
     What did the sandpiper do with his legs when
he flew?

FIGURE 1–1

and I worked together to find books in which the story was riveting and the prose manageable. Helping Rachel make reading choices was a yearlong effort.

Not surprising, Rachel's first writing effort was a letter to the Nike Corporation requesting free posters of runners. Because she was so dedicated to running, I encouraged the project and worked with her on it. Given the nature of the project, this seemed an ideal opportunity to teach Rachel how to use persuasion. Following several writing conferences with me, she wrote numerous drafts. However, no draft was substantially different from her original. Although she wanted the free posters, the Nike letter became Rachel's way of avoiding other writing projects. Finally she and I set a deadline when the letter was either to be mailed or filed in her writing folder. Once she finished the letter and sent it, Rachel was without a writing project.

At about this time the faculty, as part of our yearlong study of immigration in social studies, decided to publish an all-school magazine dedicated to family stories. I discussed the publication with my students in a minilesson and conducted subsequent minilessons around a family story I was writing about my Irish ancestors. Rachel talked about family stories with her parents and decided to tell the story of her father's trip to Europe between his junior and senior year of college, which she did, in page after page of factual information: her father went to Bruges, Assisi, the Swiss Alps, Geneva, Paris. Clearly, I needed to find a way to help her find topics of her own about which she cared and into which she could breath her own voice.

During the first week of school I had introduced Rachel and her classmates to nature notebooks. (When I taught in the Oyster River School District in Durham, New Hampshire, my colleague Joan Zelonis introduced nature notebooks to me.) I began by showing my students an entry in my own notebook (see Figure 1–1) and discussing what I observed and how I recorded my observations. Then I outlined my expectations for their nature notebooks (see Figure 1–2).

Rachel, her classmates, and I observed, drew, wrote, and thought in our nature notebooks each week. Once a week my students and I shared and discussed our work. I read the notebooks but did not write in them, (I have since changed that practice because Rachel, in particular, craved written feedback.)

I was looking for a way in, a key to help Rachel in her writing. Around the middle of October I sat down with her notebook and examined her work thus far. Rachel's voice was on these pages. I could see what interested her, where her authority lay, what her questions were (see Figure 1–3).

The following day, Rachel and I looked at her nature notebook together. She said, "I really like working in this notebook. I usually work longer than an hour each week. Working in the notebook makes me notice [things like] how many details there really are in the veins of a leaf."

"Rachel," I said, "I think you have writing topics here."

Rachel was surprised, "You think so?"

"Why don't you start bringing your notebook to writing workshop," I suggested. "You can either write in it or read it to see if you can find ideas for your writing."

Rachel brought the notebook, but she did not begin to use it to develop

Susan Benedict

4

Suean Benedict
The Center for Teaching and Learning
Edgecomb, Maine

EXPECTATIONS FOR YOUR NATURE NOTEBOOK

*Set aside **at least** an hour each week to **observe, draw, think,** and **write** about nature.

*Go outside in daylight to work in your Nature Notebook unless your observations can best be made in the dark.

*For each entry write the date (top right hand corner). Note the time of day, your location, the weather and any other pertinent information.

*Consider choosing an area of interest on which to focus for a time. Or return to objects you've observed before during the course of the year.

*Really **look, listen, smell,** and **touch.**

*Make more than one sketch or drawing. **Experiment** with different points of view and different kinds of drawing (e.g. contour, gesture) and writing (e.g. narrative, poetry).

*Your observations, drawing, thinking, and writing are all important. Move back and forth among these activities as you work.

*Remember: entries to your notebook are not final drafts. Don't censor yourself. Pieces of writing or art projects may emerge from your entries.

FIGURE 1–2

writing projects. I waited. Outside, the trees, except for the tenacious oaks, lost their leaves. The world muted to tones of brown and rust. At home Rachel watched the leaves dry and recorded in her notebook that they crinkled beneath her feet. The weather patterns changed, and the brilliant October sky gave way to frequent grays as November approached. Rachel observed the final flocks of migrating birds fly south.

When a killing frost struck the area, Rachel collected the leaves and golden flowers of witch hazel. She studied them. The next day she brought her nature notebook to writing workshop. She showed me her work (Figure 1–4) and said, "I think I can write a poem about this." Rachel drafted her poem. For the first time she realized that her wonderings, her drawings, and her keen observational skills were tools she could use when she wrote (Figure 1–5 is the final version of the poem).

Writing still did not come easily for Rachel. Each line, each word, was painfully extracted from her experience, examined, changed, and reexamined. But she recognized that words should enhance and complement the images she captured with her drawing pencil. Just as art could express things she was unable to capture with words, words could tell the story she was unable to convey through pictures alone.

My students and I shared the good fortune that as director of the

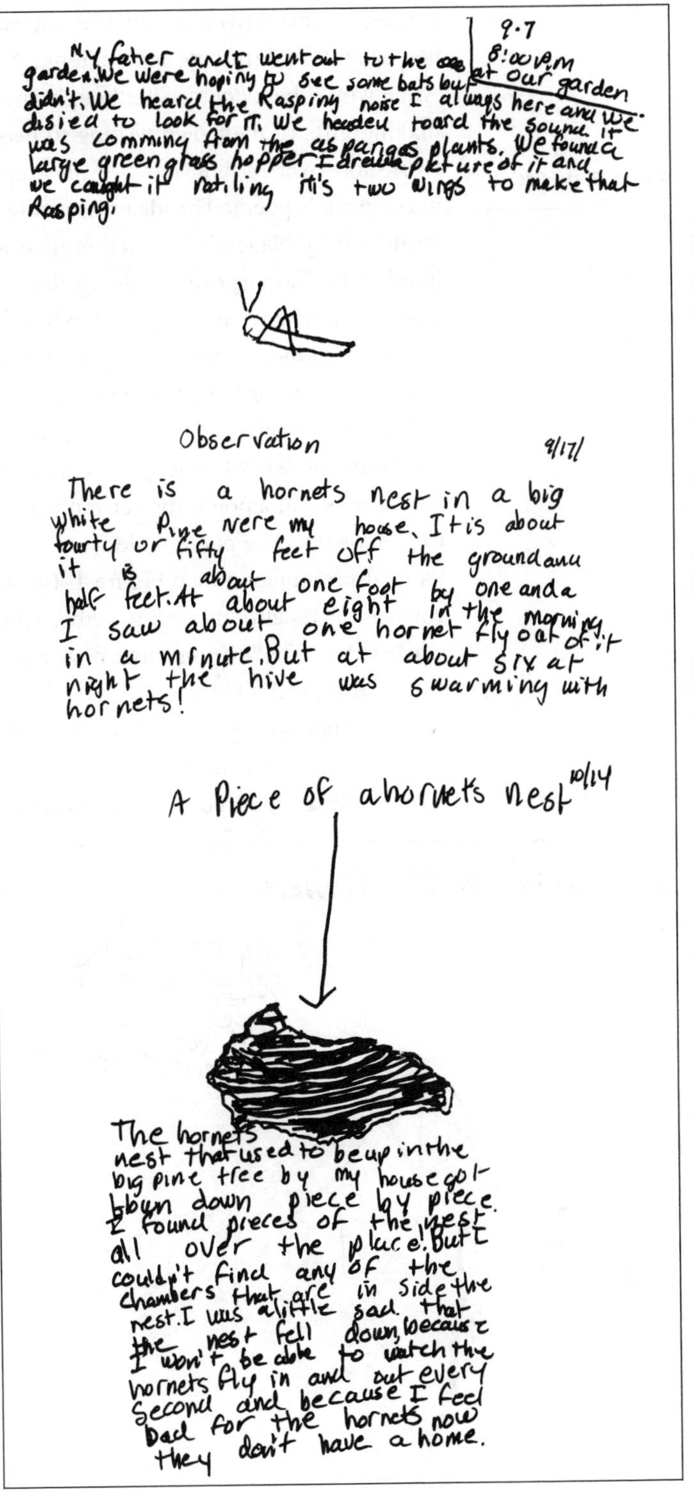

My father and I went out to the garden. We were hoping to see some bats but we didn't. We heard the Rasping noise I always here at our garden. 9·7 8:00 P.M. at our garden. We dasied to look for it. We headed toard the sound it was comming from the asparagus plants. We found a large green grass hopper I drew a pkture of it and we caught it ratiling it's two wings to make that Rasping.

Observation   9/17/

There is a hornets nest in a big white Pine nere my house. It is about fourty or fifty feet off the ground an it is about one and a half feet. At about one foot by one and a about eight in the morning I saw about one hornet fly out of it in a minute. But at about six at night the hive was swarming with hornets!

A Piece of a hornets nest 10/14

The hornets nest that used to be up in the big pine tree by my house got bbwn down piece by piece. I found pieces of the nest all over the place. But I couldn't find any of the chambers that are inside the nest. I was a little sad that the nest fell down because I won't be able to watch the hornets fly in and out every second and because I feel bad for the hornets now they don't have a home.

FIGURE 1–3

Center, Nancie Atwell conducts demonstration lessons in the classrooms. With her daughter's birthday approaching, Nancie decided that one of her gifts to Anne would be a poem. She thought my students would respond to the idea of making gifts of their own writing to people they love and came to our writing workshop over several days to do a series of minilessons during which she wrote Anne's poem. The idea was a new one for my students. No one was more motivated by Nancie's instruction than Rachel. Because she was practical and liked to find a purpose for doing things, Rachel always made her own gifts. Now a whole new venue opened to her. And since winter and early spring were times for birthday and other special occasions in her family life, Rachel had real audiences for whom to write, draw, and paint.

On the morning of January 3, as she and her mother headed out their driveway for school, Rachel saw her first cardinal of the winter. That day in class she began a poem for her mother's birthday. She labored over "Cardinal" for six weeks. The poem underwent dramatic changes from its earliest draft to its final presentation (see Figure 1–6). Along the way Rachel read poetry. She considered repetition, strong verbs, similes, verbal images, line breaks, and white space. The writing came first. Her graphic representation, to amplify her words, followed.

Later that spring, several weeks before teacher appreciation day, Rachel asked me what my favorite flower was. On the specified day she presented me with a delicate colored pencil drawing and this poem:

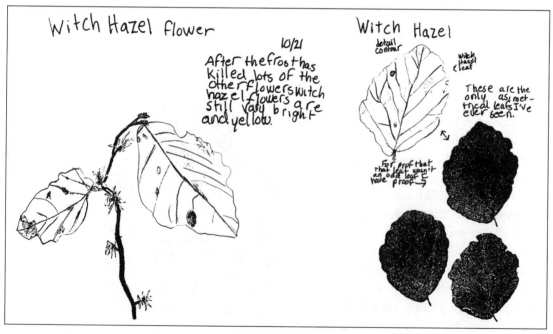

FIGURE 1–4

DAFFODILS

Golden bells ring out their beauty
lighting any day with their
sun bright blossoms
begging spring with
a fresh new start
Delicate yellow petals circle
orange crowns
long slender stems
cradle jewels
almost too precious to hold

Drawing Rachel In

7

In early March Rachel talked to me about the Hebrew class she had insisted her parents allow her to take. From what I could gather, she had a young, enthusiastic teacher who was passionately interested in the Holocaust and asked the class to read *Seed of Sarah* (Isaacson 1990). Rachel was fascinated by the subject but lamented over the difficulty of the book. Her parents and I both helped her interpret the text and encouraged her to let her teacher know

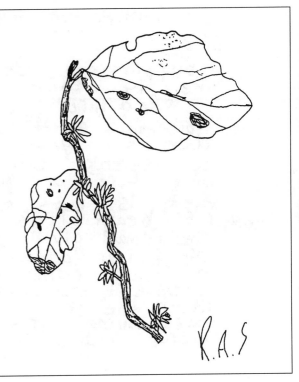

Witch Hazel

Asymmetrical leaves
delicate tiny flowers
with thread-like petals
the color of polished gold

After all the other flowers
have been devoured
by frigid weather

Witch hazel is bright
as ever

R.A.S

FIGURE 1–5

1/11

Poem / Cardinals

Red strecks racing
rarly the wind
seen
serecas masked ~~fly~~ faces
and a bright
beak~~s~~.

1/17

continuing my cardinal Poem

it's Bill
^ Surprisingly stout ~~─────~~
He is often spoken as
"Red Bird"
You may ~~catch~~ see one darting
across your yard like
a streak of flam.? streak
of fire? a Blaze? Basicly their
diet is ~~bugs~~ and berrys. there
song as beautiful as there ~~color~~ coat.
The female giving the aperance.
of Being Faded.Red Flash. A flash
of red coming to veiw one
moment dissapearing the next.
About the size of a Robin. Black
mask couing it's face as if he
were hiding something.

FIGURE 1–6

Cardinal
Red strecks racing the Wind
In winter, like
~~**Blood**~~
~~**Against the snow**~~ or

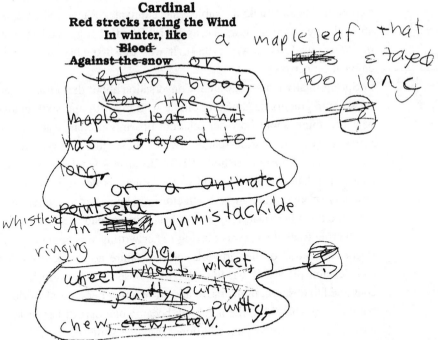

a maple leaf that
~~its~~ stayed
too long

~~But not blood,~~
~~then~~ like a
maple leaf that
has stayed to
long, or a ~~animated~~
whistleing ~~pointseta~~
ringing An ~~its~~ unmistackible
song.
wheet, wheet, wheet,
purtty, purtty,
chew, ~~chew,~~ chew. purtty,

Cardinal

Red streak
races the wind in winter
like a maple leaf
that stayed too long

Red bird
whistles
an unmistakable
ringing song

Red flash
comes into view
one moment
disappears the next

Red berries
cradled in his stout beak
he darts across your yard
a blaze of fire

Racing the wind

Cardinal
Red streaks
race the wind in winter
like a maple leaf
that stayed too long
'Red Bird'
whistles
a unmistakable
ringing song
A flash of red
comes to view
one moment,
disappears the next
With red berries
cradled in their stout beaks
they dart across your yard
a blaze of fire
Racing the wind

how difficult it was for her to read. When Rachel still struggled, her parents intervened with the teacher, and the book was put away for the time being. But a chord had been struck; the subject had captivated Rachel. She wanted to know about the treatment of Jews during World War II. I suggested she read *Number the Stars,* by Lois Lowry (1989). It was the first challenging book Rachel enjoyed on her own.

Spring finally came to Maine. Conversation about the school's new addition for seventh graders became a hot topic with my fifth and sixth graders. Rachel began to think about how her relationships might change as her older class-mates moved into middle school. Two of those girls had read *Are You There, God? It's Me, Margaret* (Blume 1970). Because Rachel wanted to know about changing relationships, she read it, too. Rachel's desire to know "stuff" was probably stronger than any other factor in helping her to plunge into and stick with books on her own. Rachel was becoming a reader.

The role Rachel's art was playing in her writing was changing too. Initially, Rachel depended on her artwork and her nature notebook to explore, define, and develop pieces of writing. Her own observations were her source. She continued to observe, think, draw, and write about her natural world each week, but the work she did in the notebook became one part of her collected experi-ence. She began to develop additional research skills.

In order to write "The Mark" Rachel read extensively about humpback whales, watched films about whales, and went on a whale watch. Research and writing were not linear activities for her. Because she readily saw images, Rachel used image making to make sense of her learning and her world. As she read and recorded facts, she simultaneously worked to capture images (see Figure 1–7).

Once captured, Rachel collected the images in her poem.

THE MARK

Aquatic acrobats playfully
breach and slap
their huge flippers
against gleaming water.

They crash, and create
a thundering echo
through
the sea.

These deep divers
serenade the sea with

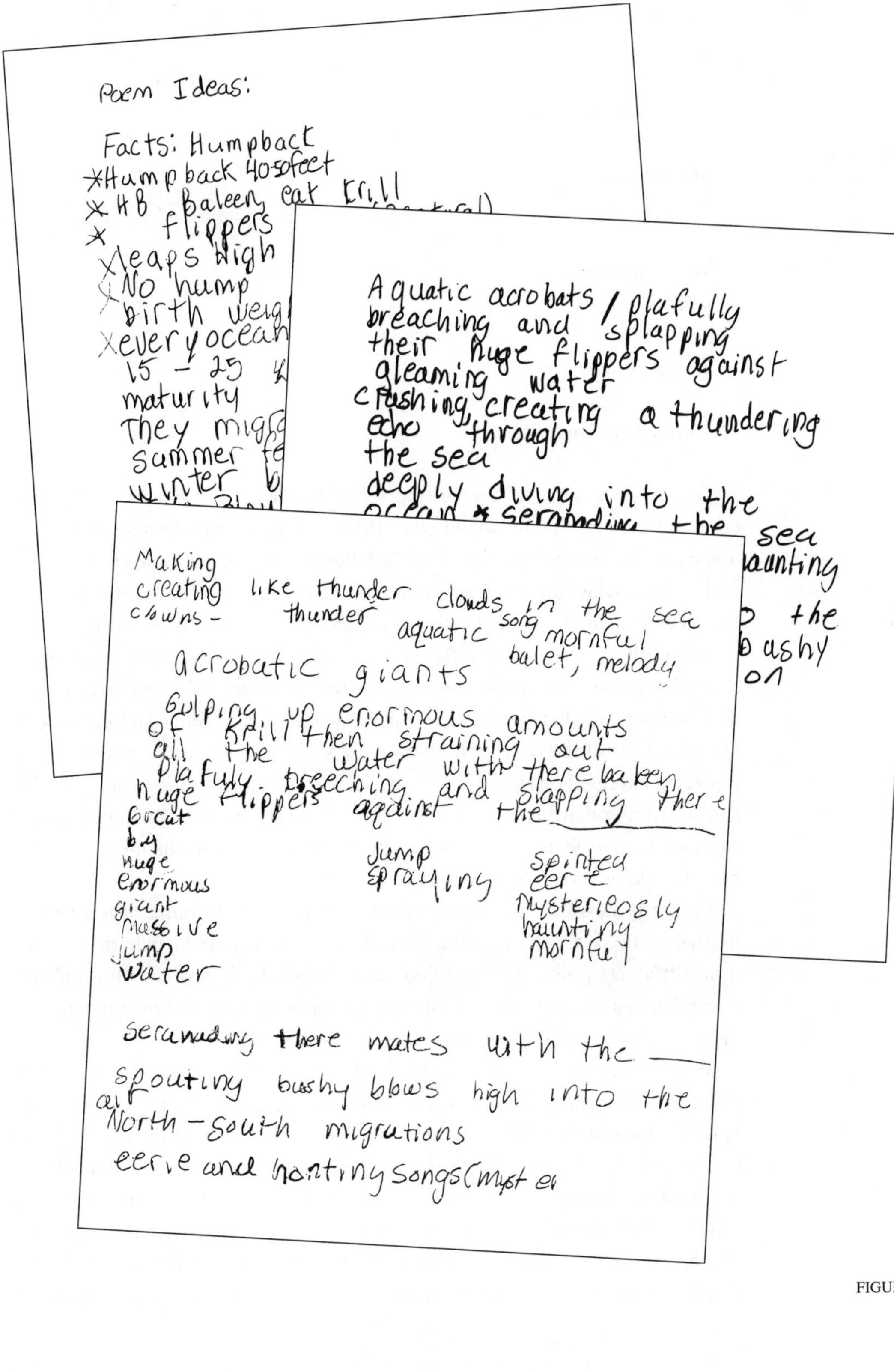

Poem Ideas:

Facts: Humpback
*Humpback 40-50 feet
* HB Baleen eat krill (central)
* flippers
* leaps high
* No hump
* birth weig
* every ocean
15 - 25 k
maturity
They migr
summer t
winter b

Aquatic acrobats / plafully
breaching and slapping
their huge flippers against
gleaming water
crashing creating a thundering
echo through
the sea
deeply diving into the
ocean * serenading the sea
haunting
the
bushy
on

Making
creating like thunder clouds in the sea
clowns-   thunder   aquatic song mornful
                                 balet, melody
    acrobatic giants
Gulping up enormous amounts
of krill then straining out
all the water with there baleen
Plafuly breeching and slapping there
huge flippers against the _____
Great
big
huge   Jump   spinted
enormous   spraying   eere
giant   mysterieosly
massive   haunting
Jump   mornful
water

serenadwing there mates with the ____
spouting bushy blows high into the air
North - South migrations
eerie and hantiny songs (myst er

FIGURE 1-7

mysterious, haunting
melodies.

Powerfully they swim
to the surface
of the frigid
Arctic Ocean—

Then, spouting
a bushy blow
leave a mark
on the horizon—

Mark of the humpback.

Once she recognized her writing tools, Rachel found her own way. She collected images. She drew and recorded the images that surrounded her. It is not surprising that poetry captivated her. Poems offered her an avenue through which she could flow between verbal and visual image making. Her passions for accuracy, simplicity, and conciseness are the basic tenets of poetry.

All of my students bring different tools with them to the blank page. Some bring description, metaphor, story structure, and characters they have met in their reading. Rachel brought the natural world, her appetite and capacity to know, and her ability to capture her observations graphically. If I had allowed Rachel to express herself only verbally, she might still be writing letters to Nike and rewriting other people's stories. She still might not recognize that people write about their lives, their passions, their wondering. And she might not have been moved to read to discover other people's passions.

I recently heard a naturalist speak about butterflies. In order to learn about butterflies, he said, you must find them. The best way to find a butterfly is when it is still a caterpillar. And you find caterpillars where they eat. But different caterpillars eat different things. Most of us know we can find the monarchs in the milkweed patch. But can we find a hoary comma?

We can learn about our students, and help them learn about their world, through their writing. However, not all of our students are able to raise their voices in the genres of Western literature. As in our search for the elusive hoary comma, we need to find what feeds each student's heart and mind. Rachel's art is the conduit through which she filters her knowledge and the world. It is there I first encountered her. We may find other students in the science lab, at the end of a hammer, or reeling in a fishing line. How fortunate for Rachel and for me that I offered the nature notebook as one way my students could learn about their world and one way that I could learn about them. But what about the carpenters and scientists? We need to offer our students alternate ways through which they can learn about their world, through which we can learn about them.

Writing is the way I learn. Writing about Rachel has helped me know her in a way I wouldn't have otherwise. Rachel is now my student for a second year, and as this fall turns to winter we are both still drawing, writing, and learning, together.

References

Atwell, Nancie. 1987. *In the Middle: Writing, Reading, and Learning with Adolescents*. Portsmouth, NH: Boynton/Cook.

Blume, Judy. 1970. *Are You There, God? It's Me, Margaret*. New York: Bradbury.

Isaacson, Judith Magyar. 1990. *Seed of Sarah*. Urbana: University of Illinois Press.

Lowry, Lois. 1989. *Number the Stars*. Boston: Houghton Mifflin.

Murray, Donald. 1984. *Write to Learn*. New York: Holt, Rinehart, and Winston.

Rylant, Cynthia. 1985. "Shells." In *Every Living Thing*. New York: Bradbury.

2

Widening the Frame: Reading, Writing, and Art in Learning

Karen Ernst

I drew Megan into my sketch journal as she worked in the artists workshop (see Figure 2–1). *Large as Life* (Finzel 1991) was propped on the table, and she was using oil pastels to copy a plant from the opened pages of the book. Mary Kate was creating a picture with crayons and markers, getting her inspiration from a postcard reproduction of a painting by Georgia O'Keeffe. Margaux and Samantha sat on the rug with their sketch journals, drawing each other and a plant that brightened the counter of the art room. Several students carefully selected papers from the collage cart, while others mixed paints on their individual palettes. Kevin and Josh pushed and turned their clay, preparing to sculpt it into something from their imagination. David sat alone and wrote in his journal about his process of making a clay figure of van Gogh's "The Postman Roulin." Taped classical music played in the background while I dispensed paint at the paint cart and cut more clay for the sculptors.

The artists workshop at Kings Highway, a K–4 elementary school, enables students to select their topics and media, requires that students come to their one-hour-per-week art class with an idea, and teaches them to be responsible for their materials. The workshop approach demands that I develop an order, a routine, and a structure within which children will learn about technique and be able to create within boundaries that nevertheless encourage risk taking. It places thinking and learning, not product, at the center of what children do. Art and literature provide a context for learning, and professional artists and authors are models for ideas and techniques. Including writing as an integral process in the artists workshop encourages children to think about their work and provides a way for them to express the thinking behind their pictures and projects. In this workshop, reading, writing, and art work together to widen the frame for expression and meaning. Together they open the imagination to new possibilities.

I came to this position—"elementary art specialist"—looking for possible

Megan knew which book she needed to finish her picture. As she got her own materials she propped pages of the book made a burst of flowers in the room. She chats with Ann, on the other side of the book, but mostly concentrates on her picture

FIGURE 2–1

ways art could connect to whole learning. As a former middle school English teacher, I understood how the writers/readers workshop approach, influenced by Graves (1983), Calkins (1986), and Atwell (1987), could empower children to express inner thoughts and feelings and could help create a community of learners in the classroom. My strong belief in this process led me to develop a parallel approach—the artists workshop. I began by developing a routine the children could anticipate each week, and told them it was their responsibility to come to art with ideas for their work. I wanted this workshop to be theirs, not focused on "projects" I invented. I am convinced that this workshop approach has propelled students to read, look, write, express, and experience things in new ways. At Kings Highway art has a place central to learning.

Structure and Routine: Community Within Boundaries

Karen Ernst

Structure and routine are essential to the workshop. Each week when the classroom teacher brings the class to the artists workshop, the children stop at the door to read my message on the easel. The subtext is always, You have come here to continue and extend your learning, your reading and writing. What we ask children to do tells them what we think is important. The message usually ends with "meet me on the rug" and it is there that we begin—reading a picture book, looking at the work of an artist, discussing the work of students from across the grade levels, or holding an "artist's share," in which a student volunteers to share her or his work in progress and get responses. This ten-minute meeting on the rug helps focus our thinking about art and literacy and helps students get ideas for their own work. It is our rehearsal for learning; it shows my students that thinking is as important here as product.

Our rug activity is followed by a minilesson in which I show students a particular technique or medium, focus on a routine in the workshop, describe how to clean up more efficiently, or demonstrate a way to write about the pictures they make. I then ask each student to tell me his or her artwork idea as well as the medium he or she will use that day: oil pastel, marker, crayon, pen, paint, clay, or collage. The number of choices increases gradually. Students use a particular medium only after a minilesson has focused on techniques of using it. Knowing that they need to come to the workshop with an idea helps students look at the world around them and at their own experiences as possible sources of ideas for pictures, projects, and writing. Thus they connect what we do in art to their whole learning and to their lives.

Each student keeps a portfolio of work and a notebook or sketch journal in which he or she writes about the work; both are reviewed with parents several times during the year. These portfolios and journals become a record of the work students are doing and help us connect mistakes with successes, process with product. The children work toward all-school exhibitions several times a year for which each student selects a work that is placed on the hallway bulletin boards.

These routines—indeed everything I do as a teacher—reflect what I believe is important in the classroom. I keep a sketch journal in which I draw my students as they work, make classroom observations, take notes on conversations with my students, and reflect on my classroom experiences. This makes me a learner, makes my students my informants, and models my work as an artist and writer. We read picture books to see how words and pictures work together to tell a story, we look at professional artworks to learn their creator's techniques, and we talk about the work of students across the grades (learning from each other is essential). All of this creates a classroom community, enriches the school community, and encourages apprenticeships in learning—between student and teacher, between students and other students, and between students and professional artists and writers.

The minilessons at the beginning of the workshop are critical. Pointing out all the things that can help students get ideas—books, the classroom gallery of art reproductions, physical objects, nature—is as important as showing how to use watercolors, oil pastels, and clay. Repeating minilessons on the classroom routines, how I expect them to use their time, the kind of talk about work and process that is appropriate in the workshop, and how to clean up responsibly and quickly help make the workshop a place of focused work.

Questioning my students about process and asking them to write about what they learn or discover pushes the workshop's focus toward thinking and learning and away from what a picture or project looks like. Their writing constantly informs me about their progress. Encouraging students to experiment and discover leads them to new possibilities for what they can create, instills in them a willingness to take risks, and gives them a sense of confidence in their work.

Seeing Meaning: Connecting Art and Writing

My students' pictures take on deeper and more integrated meaning for me through their writing. Each student in grades one through four has an artists notebook, which is kept in the portfolio in the artists workshop. Many children also have sketch journals, which they carry back and forth from their classroom to the artists workshop and often take home as well. The classroom teacher assigns both writing and drawing in these sketch journals, thus helping extend art across the curriculum. Writing as part of the artists workshop and as an extension of it encourages students to examine process, focus on thinking, and extend the boundaries of form to include poems, descriptions, reflections.

The children reveal where they get ideas and how art expresses meaning. A second grader wrote at the end of her art class, "I made a picture that is like Matisse's. I am also in the middle of another Matisse picture which I hope I will finish next time we have art." In these brief statements she shows where the idea for her picture came from, what she is planning for the next art class, and that she is involved in her own project, not one "assigned" by me. The work of artists and authors inspires student work. As she and other students share their writing with me and with each other, more ideas are generated, more apprenticeships initiated, and more possibilities seen.

Sometimes I raise questions about the elements of the workshop and ask the students to respond in writing. On the issue of "copying" ideas from another artist, Tyler, a third grader, wrote:

> *I think copying helps set your mind free. I think I kind of copied Ms. Olbrych's picture because I almost used the same color for the water in the stream in the field. I also think copying is good because you get really good ideas. In my picture I put very tall, tall grass and a stream.*

Tyler's writing helped me understand the benefits of "copying," whether imitating another student, a teacher, or the masters. Inspired by a teacher's picture displayed on the "teacher bulletin board" in the artists workshop, Tyler was learning technique, making comparisons, and describing his own picture.

Connecting art and writing has widened children's ability to write descriptively and poetically about what they see. Frank, a fourth grader, vividly evokes his picture with his words:

> *Today I drew a picture of the mountains in Colorado. It is like this: You sit back in a row boat and the mountains are ahead. They look like huge rocky Hershey Kisses that the tops are dipped in frosting. You can imagine the wind in your face. The cold ice on your hand. You are in the great Rockies!*

The picture gives him a topic for writing and his writing takes him beyond the picture as he describes the feeling of being there. He uses simile to make his readers see what he saw.

Typically, we write after clean-up, during the last ten minutes of class. If the classroom teacher is incorporating art into the writers workshop, students often also write about their art work when they return to the classroom. Knowing that they will write pushes students to be conscious of their process and to pay attention to what they see. The other teachers and I question and model. We often say, Try not just to say what you did, or urge, Write more!

I often ease the students into their period of silent writing with questions:

- What do you see in your picture?
- What do you feel as you look at your picture?
- What is the story in or beyond your picture?
- If you went inside your picture, what would you find?
- What inspired you?
- What are your plans for the next workshop?
- What surprised you or what did you discover as you worked?

I ask my students to use words to paint a picture or to read a painting by telling what they see there.

In this workshop where writing, reading, and art are partners in learning, the processes interrelate and overlap. Here are some ways I tell my students they can combine art, reading, and writing:

- Look through picture books to get ideas for pictures and writing.
- Read a picture book. Notice techniques of the illustrator. Always ask, How can I get the same effect?
- Read a book. Listen for the word images.
- Read a book for an idea for a picture.
- Read a picture book to examine a technique.
- Respond to a book through pictures or writing.
- Copy a picture from a book to learn from the artist/illustrator.
- Close your eyes while you listen to a story or poem and watch the pictures in your imagination.
- Look at a painting of an artist. Describe what you see, what you feel, what story comes to mind, what the artist does that interests you.
- Copy the work of an artist.
- Share your own picture, ideas, and meanings.
- Sketch and write about the work of another student.
- Use language to create a picture of what you made.
- Look at your own picture, write what you see and feel, and give it a title.

The Challenge of Choice: Learning from the Tensions

The balance between structure and letting go in the workshop is a constant tension for me and challenges me as a teacher. Even though choice is central to my teaching, at times I encounter a picture I do not understand. Sally, for example, worked hard on a collage of flowers she had cut from a piece of wallpaper, then scribbled oil pastels in the corners. As she worked, she chatted away with her friends at her table. Discouraged by Sally's product, I began wondering about the viability of providing so many choices, wondering if as a fourth grader she was learning enough technique. My wondering went into my own journal as I drew Sally and others as they worked. I asked everyone in the class to put into words what she or he had learned or discovered that day. Sally's writing surprised me:

I tried something new today, collage. It was wallpaper. It was great. I feel different about my pictures because I express my feelings, like on my collage. I did flowers and that's how I felt, happy, excited, and confident in myself for what I did today! I feel confident in myself when I work and I feel good when I'm finished. I like all of my pictures.

Sally had taken a risk. She had finally tried collage, but not until she was ready. Her words helped me understand what I could not see or interpret in her picture. She reminded me that making choices and taking charge of one's own work is empowering.

By watching closely and questioning, letting my students be my informants, I have come to understand the kinds of responsibilities that are nurtured by giving students the ability to make choices and the challenges I need to meet as the teacher who provides these choices. I must teach conventions as well as possibilities, must model my own work as a learner. Choices open all kinds of possibilities in learning, both the children's and mine.

Reading as Artists: Children's Literature in the Artists Workshop

Just as students read as writers in a writers workshop and write as readers in a readers workshop, my students read as artists or paint as writers in the artists workshop. They read to get ideas, they draw to read, and they respond to literature in words and pictures. We read picture books as one of our rehearsal activities, and students borrow books from the workshop library, called "the library of ideas," from which to copy or to get ideas.

FIGURE 2–2

Katie sat on the corner of the rug, her eyes on a page in *Large as Life* (Finzel 1991), carefully copying an intricate painting of an owl perched on a limb. For five weekly meetings, while the other fourth graders worked and chatted at their tables, Katie drew. (Figure 2–2 is her completed drawing.) Other students passed by, admired her work, and then went on with their own projects. Having made a choice in her work, Katie undertook it with an intensity that could not be assigned.

Katie's attention to detail as well as her patience became a model for her classmates. After doing her version of the owl in oil pastels, Margaret wrote:

> *I was inspired by Katie's picture of an owl. I decided, I think, three weeks ago that I would make some owls too. I think when I find something that I like I try to draw it again and again, doing each in a different perspective. Last year it was a lion and now it is an owl. As I look around the room I get lots of ideas but I only stick with one.*

Margaret's awareness of her own process showed me the power of students' selecting their own projects, even when they copy someone else's idea or choose the same topic over and over. Fourth graders, like professional artists, learn from each other and learn from repeating an idea using new perspectives.

David, also a fourth grader, copied an illustration from a book into his sketch journal. Even though his intention was simply to become better at drawing, he found that working so closely with the illustration heightened his interest in reading the book. He described in detail how he made the picture and where he got his idea. He added, "I am now reading *Tom Sawyer*. My picture inspired me to read the book. I am glad and I really like the book so far. I hope all of my pictures are as good as this." David had become his own teacher.

Students begin to make their own connections in learning, they develop their own ability to assess themselves, and they take charge of their own work and progress. When literature, art, and writing are combined and there is a focus on thinking in the workshop, I often find that students can describe these connections in the clearest terms. When I asked a fourth-grade class about any connections they saw between reading, writing, and art, Frank wrote,

I think artists workshop, writers workshop, and readers workshop work together in many ways. One of them is that sometimes writing helps me think of pictures to make. Another is that when I read, pictures come into my head and they are sometimes so beautiful I have to write them down. And when I write them down I remember it so clearly I make a picture of it.

For our library's annual book fair some students made pictures that called attention to their favorite books. Some students copied the cover, others made collages that captured a specific incident. Nick's favorite book was a chapter book with no pictures. He did a careful line drawing of the cover and then glued down a circle made from tiny pieces of torn shiny paper. Inside the circle he wrote, "I picked this book because of the good pictures. Even though it had no pictures, I saw them in the words."

The Pictures in the Words: Sketching a Text

A class of fourth graders sat on the rug, ready for our rehearsal. I had chosen to read *The Same Wind* (Killion 1982) because of the feelings aroused by its imagery. I suggested that as I read they could either look at the illustrations in the book or close their eyes and look at the pictures the words prompted in their imagination.

Ben, a student who was very successful at expressing himself through pictures and less confident about reading and writing, raised his hand. "Can I sketch as you read the words?" As I read, "Are you the same wind that cries over the southern swamps, moving the dark murky waters where the cypress trees wade to their knees, and the alligators sleep, slapping their tales," he drew an alligator emerging from the swamp grass, showed the mountains, sun, and sky washing across the page.

Watching Ben sketch, I thought again how important it is to stay open to new possibilities, to listen to my students, to be flexible. A workshop that supports choice must also support risk taking and trust for teacher and students. I offered my remaining classes an additional option: " sketch while you listen."

Reading an Exhibition, Picturing a Text, Writing Meaning

Students sat quietly in the hallway, their eyes focused on the pictures in the all-school exhibition (see Figure 2–3). They sketched a picture because they liked it, because they were interested in how the artist made it, or perhaps to remember ideas for their own future work. After they drew, they wrote about why they "read" this picture, why they chose to focus on it. All-school exhibitions are opportunities to learn, gather ideas, and respond to the other students in the school. They become a form of assessment, they inform the wider community of the school—parents, teachers, visitors—and they present the students' work in progress. Working toward an exhibition heightens productivity and widens the interchange among students at all grade levels. The keen awareness of audience alters the kind of work a student does.

Cary was interested in a drawing by Michael. Michael typically drew scenes from wars—airplanes dropping bombs, men with guns shooting at each other. For this exhibition he had drawn a woodland scene: a log cabin, a hunter chasing a rabbit, a fisherman, although he did include an airliner partially hidden behind a huge tree. Cary took her interpretation of Michael's piece back to the artists workshop and used oil pastels to continue her work. In her drawing she eliminated all of Michael's objects, focused on the landscape, and added a sunset. In her sketch the tree from Michael's picture became an oasis of trees. She worked deliberately and searched for just the right color for her sunset sky.

When Cary brought her picture to me, she said, "I think this is my best so

FIGURE 2–3

far." This was typically Cary. She worked with intensity and confidence and was always ready with a personal critique. She was not satisfied with the sky, so we went to "the library of Ideas." I showed her a few pages in *The Foolish Rabbit's Big Mistake* (Martin & Young 1985) to let her see another possibility. As we searched and talked, I told Cary about our librarian's idea for the book fair: she wanted to display pictures that had been created in response to a favorite book. I showed her how I would respond to one of my favorite passages. Cary listened and then admitted, "I couldn't do it like that. I love the entire Narnia series, not one passage, or page, or book."

She then decided that this landscape—the one in oil pastel, the one in which she'd had to struggle to achieve the sky, the one based on Michael's landscape in the exhibition—showed her response to the Narnia series. I sent her to her artist's notebook to explain how:

> *Look at the deep pastel brown of the trees. It looks all mysterious and real. Yet not as if real in places that we know of. Real as in places we have not explored yet. Real like Narnia. Mystical, strange, unknown, and yet known. Always teasing you to challenge yourself, to go into the unknown, to discover all its passages and doors.*

There is no separation between reading, writing, and art. Each member of this learning community, whether student or teacher, depends on the other members for ideas, collaboration, attention, and response. Cary's idea began with Michael and the exhibition, Michael's idea had been propelled by the knowledge of going public with his work, and my interpretation of the librarian's idea changed and broadened as I helped Cary, made a suggestion, and listened to what she said in response.

Challenging Ourselves

Students chatted about their individual projects to the accompaniment of Mozart. Some lined up at the paint cart where I dispensed paint, while others worked at their tables on collage, clay, and oil pastel. Three girls huddled on the rug: one wrote and sketched in her journal, another copied an illustration from a book, and the third sprawled on the floor as she stared at a reproduction of a painting by a professional artist.

Mary Kate wrote in her artist's notebook,

> *When I look at my picture it makes me feel like it was done by Georgia O'Keeffe. I wrote a poem: Look down. Do you see what I see? Do you feel what I feel? The blazing red, blue, yellow, white. Makes me feel warm and happy.*

Marc had spent several weeks working on a copy of van Gogh's "Starry Night," using markers:

Karen Ernst

24

Today I really challenged myself. I drew a picture called Starry Night. The part that was most challenging was the houses because on the picture there were about one hundred houses. So instead I made them into bushes.

Students know their boundaries in this artists workshop, a workshop in which literature, art, and writing work together. Within these boundaries, established through routine and structure, they begin to push hard against what they can do, to discover how they can best express themselves, and to feel secure enough to take risks to discover new ideas, new connections, and new meaning. They begin to assess their own work and set new limits for themselves. They challenge what they know and what they can accomplish.

Surprise is part of the process of discovery. A student like Mary Kate may choose a professional artist like O'Keeffe as her distant mentor. Marc and students like him clearly use art and literature for ideas but take charge, challenging themselves to make those ideas their own or to deal with problems as they work. David draws to become interested in reading. Nick sees pictures in the words. Ben's expertise in making pictures makes him a teacher, a respected member of a community where pictures are valued as a form of expression; in return he is challenged to become a better reader and writer.

Doors open for both teacher and students as we collaborate, copy, exchange ideas, and change what happens in the workshop based on what we learn. When multiple forms of expression are honored, when teachers observe and listen to their students, when students become the informants for change, the connections between reading, writing, and art are ever powerful and ever changing. The frame of learning widens. The picture of learning in that wider frame includes more children, more success, more learning—and endless possibilities.

References

Atwell, N. 1987. *In the Middle: Writing, Reading, and Learning with Adolescents.* Portsmouth, NH: Boynton/Cook.

Calkins, L. M. 1986. *The Art of Teaching Writing.* Portsmouth, NH: Heinemann.

Finzel, J. 1991. *Large as Life.* New York: Lothrop, Lee & Shepard.

Graves, D. (1983). *Writing: Teachers and Children at Work.* Portsmouth, NH: Heinemann.

Killion, B. 1982. *The Same Wind.* Illustrated B. B. Falk. New York: Harper's Children's Books.

Lewis, C. S. 1951. *The Chronicles of Narnia.* New York: Harper's.

Martin, R., and E. Young. 1985. *The Foolish Rabbit's Big Mistake.* New York: Putnam.

Twain, M. 1946. *The Adventures of Tom Sawyer.* Kingsport, TN: Grossett and Dunlop.

3

Writing Pictures, Painting Words:
Artists Notebooks
in Literacy Workshops

Nancy Winterbourne

As a teacher who is also an aspiring artist and writer, I am fascinated by the creative connection between text and image in the development of young children's literacy. I've found that encouraging children to integrate drawing and writing helps them develop their communication abilities in all of the language arts. Two years ago, I decided to take my literacy program one step further by setting up a deliberate artists workshop—as opposed to my usual ad hoc version—in my self-contained second-grade classroom. I hoped to create new drawing and writing experiences for all my students. And as a teacher-researcher in my classroom, I wanted to document how this new aspect of my literacy program would affect my students' growth as writers and artists, thinkers and communicators.

The literacy workshop already established in my classroom gave the children daily opportunities to express thoughts and feelings with their writing and drawing. For several years, I have structured this workshop so that the children write in their journals every day on topics that they choose, then share their writing with each other and with me. (This sharing is done through informal writing conferences and through larger class discussions in which the author shares work and takes comments and questions from the rest of the class.) Their journals are small books made of folded-in-half typing paper, stapled on one side, with construction paper covers. When the journal pages are open, one side is designated for pictures and the other for words. I give equal emphasis to developing the processes of drawing and writing.

For some children, this hasn't been enough. Emily began the year by composing complete sentences in her journal, but she left the illustration pages blank. When I encouraged her to draw pictures to go with her story, she refused with a shake of her head and a whispered, "I can't draw anything" or "I really don't like to make pictures." Yet, several months later, after taking part in our new artists workshop, Emily's plan for an art studio included a detailed drawing

What is art?
Art is prity flowers Colors fo
everey cinde art is thinking,
making and designs. art is
inventing imagination
eney thing you wont.

we are art

FIGURE 3–1

and reflected a wonderful sense of openness in her attitude toward her own artistic life. "Art Studio Yes!!" she heads her plan, explaining:

> If I had a art room I would have tons of stuff. I would have a desk to do things with. I would have milk cartons, and things that I could use, old things, pop bottles. I would have a thinker box I would put my head in and I would see all these things and as soon as I got an idea, I would write it down. At my studio I would have everything: paper, pencils, paints, clay, glue, peg board. Everything!!!!

Participating in the artists workshop helped open up new possibilities for Emily. Most of this growth stemmed from her interactions with others in the room, through which she shared their attempts and ideas and their attitudes toward art. Her classmate Rachel was particularly influential, for Emily and for the other students. Quiet and at times reserved, Rachel revealed more of herself and her talents as the artists workshop became increasingly valued in our classroom community. In her self-portrait and definition of art (See Figure 3–1), Rachel instructed me on the importance art has for "inventing imagination" and closed with the simple yet important "We are art." Children like Emily and Rachel found a new sense of self-expression, validated their strengths as learners, explored more complex forms of written expression, and helped open my eyes to what was possible in the artists workshop.

Structuring an Artists Workshop

My interactions with Ruth Hubbard and Karen Ernst inspired me to try structuring an artists workshop in my classroom. Ruth spent two years in my classroom, exploring young children's literacy with me (Hubbard 1993). I was particularly interested in how and when children developed time elements in their writing and in how their daily observational drawings in their science journals helped them use more complex verb structures to explain the changes they saw in relation to both the past and the future. Karen's description of her elementary art classroom (Ernst 1994) modeled the close connection between text and image and sparked my own interpretation of the artists literacy workshop.

Classroom materials, space, and time were key in the way I structured my workshop. I decided to keep the activities and projects fairly simple, using materials already on hand: modeling clay, tempera, construction paper, glue, scissors, marking pens, papier mâché. As I searched for appropriate projects, I became aware of a genre of children's books devoted to the subject of art, books like *Talking With Artists* (Cummings 1992), *Matthew's Dream* (Lionni 1991), *Linnea in Monet's Garden* (Bjork 1985), *Rembrandt* (Venezia 1988), and even

Children's Crafts (Warton 1976). These books were sources of ideas for activities, as well as models for writing and image making.

Our carpeted classroom contained individual student desks, which we pushed together into different configurations over the year, sometimes pairs, sometimes clusters. Our other resources included a large storage cupboard and a sink. For a few of the messier projects, like finger painting, we used two larger tables on linoleum flooring in a shared area just outside the classroom.

Finding a time structure that would work for us was the most important element in making the workshop successful. The children and I needed an hour and a half of uninterrupted time each day for our literacy program, which included both a reading and a writing workshop. I planned to focus on the artists workshop for one week each month, using that ninety-minute block of time. At the beginning of the artists workshop week, I set up the art materials and explained how to use them. For example, if I set up the tempera and brushes, I told the children to cover their clothes with paint shirts and explained how to wash and care for the brushes, how to avoid mixing "muddy" colors, and how to keep the paint off their neighbors.

The artists notebooks were another important component of the workshop. I wanted my students to use their notebooks as tools to help them reflect on their process, both for planning and for noticing changes in their work. Before we began each project, I asked the children to write about and sketch how they might use the materials. I knew doing so would encourage them to plan more specifically than they might otherwise. I also wanted to provide a context that would encourage them to use future-tense verbs in their writing, something they were less likely to try on their own during regular writing workshop.

After the children had worked with the art materials, I asked them to write again, this time reflecting on how their plans had changed or on any surprises they had encountered. Besides prompting them to think about their process on a deeper level, I wanted to give them a reason to use past-tense verbs. It's important to me to provide opportunities in the curriculum to help children understand the nature of connections across time. Guided writing like this helps my students experiment with language structures they might not choose to use on their own, helps them understand their creative process, and hones relational skills that will benefit them in all areas of their learning.

Learning from the Children's Examples

Amanda's plan for and reflections about using chocolate pudding as a finger-painting medium are good examples of children's use of future- and past-tense verbs. "I think Wednesday *is going to be* the best day of my life!" she gushed. "We get to do chocolate fudge pudding but *we're going to finger paint* with it."

wednesday 5-1-92
I Made has Mouth
Biger and it's difrint
Then Thee other Parts
I Licked The Mauth
Beder Then enething
The   End

FIGURE 3–2

Her reflection focused on the mess it caused, and the unlikelihood that she'd be able to repeat the enterprise at home: "I think it *was* not ladylike, but it *was* the gooiest thing I ever *touched*. . . . But I think I *could* not *do finger painting* with chocolate pudding at home because our Mom doesn't like to clean up messes."

Another example of complex verb forms comes from Buddy's artists notebook. Figure 3–2 is his written and illustrated explanation of the figure he plans to make from modeling clay. His drawing attempts to express the three-dimensional medium in which he will be working: notice how his dinosaur's mouth opens to show teeth all around the upper jaw. In commenting on his drawing, Buddy writes that he "*made* his mouth bigger and it's different from the other parts."

Two days later, Buddy again explores how he will use modeling clay (see Figure 3–3). This time his verbs indicate the passage of time ("I *would like*," "I *have made*"), and he includes a drawing of a turtle moving away from a sophisticated three-dimensional box.

The art projects also prompted the children to use descriptive language in unusual ways. Jacob's notebook entry about his modeling clay project demonstrates his advanced use of both descriptive language and image (see Figure 3–4):

This is a whale and it is attacking a giant squid. And it is made of clay. And it is mine. I made the clay squid by five round-tipped sliders and one long wide, flat end. And an arrow head.

Jacob's ability to look at a two-dimensional drawing and then reproduce it in a sculpture is very skillful. As Jacob shifts from the reference book about whales to his clay sculpture and then to his journal writing, we see written evidence of his complex thinking and of his ability to use descriptive language to explain the shape of the squid's body.

Ray's love of math showed up in the specialized vocabulary he used in his art journal. He described the geometric shapes he used to make a construction paper house with terms he learned from math workshop: "I am going to make a cube and on top I am going to make a cone and then a square prism. It is a house." Ray boxed off the sentence *It is a house* to separate it from the sentences describing the parts, thus illustrating that geometric shapes are separate but also form a whole.

As the class worked with a new set of classroom dictionaries, Rachel became fascinated by the pictorial history of the development of individual alphabet letters. She copied ancient Egyptian and Greek letter forms onto bits of paper, and eventually she began writing notebook entries in this Greek/Egyptian "code." For example, after reading several books by Dr. Seuss, she

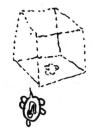

it is May 7, 1992   5-7-92
I Wod liRe to MaKe
a clay Turtle I haveMade
a clay dinusar

FIGURE 3–3

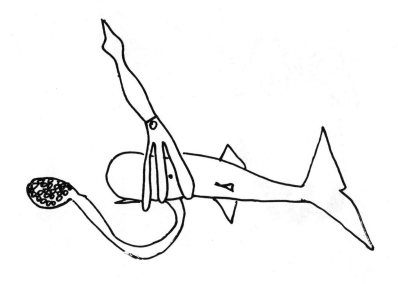

1-12-92. This a whale and it
is a tacing a ginet squid. And it
is made of clay. And it is mine
I mad the clay squid, by 5
round tip siliders and 1 long
wide, flat end. And a arruc haed

FIGURE 3–4

March 31, 1992

My Creecher is a tow heaed
Δⵙⵙ<. It is two yers ⵙⵙ7Δ.
⊅ᚱᚱΔ It I z ᚱᚱΔ. It
has ⵙⵙᚱᚱᚱ toth. ⊅ᚱᚱᚱΔ
every werd It seis startis
with Δ.

FIGURE 3–5

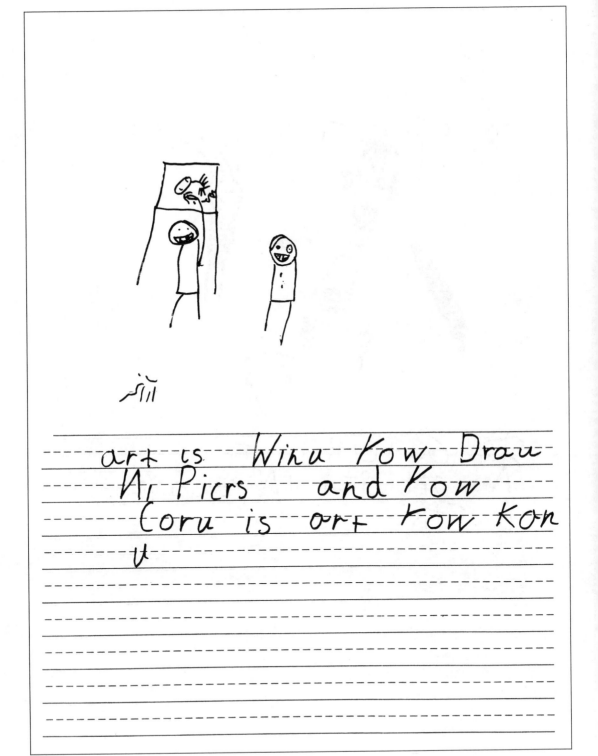

art is Wira row Draw
Hi Picrs and row
Coru is ort row Kon
u

FIGURE 3–6

IMGOTOBE
A artistiMMakene
MOStR.

FIGURE 3–7

designed an imaginary animal and wrote about it in invented spelling (see Figure 3–5), which translated into conventional spelling reads: "My creature is a two-headed dog. It is two years old. And it is red. It has one tooth. And every word it says starts with a D."

The artists workshop also had meaningful—and unexpected—benefit for my students who were struggling hardest with literacy. Making papier mâché piñatas inspired Juan to attempt his first written sentence in English. He carefully thought about each word, talked it over with a classmate, looked in his paperback spelling dictionary, and finally wrote it down: "I like to break the piñata." It took him about thirty minutes to complete the sentence and an accompanying drawing. (Later, he went back and added the Spanish tilde mark to the word piñata on his own.)

BJ's definition of art (see Figure 3–6) tells a lot about his academic struggles. He was later identified as having learning disabilities in several areas: visual-motor skills, language processing, and spatial concepts. Though there is evidence of this in the reversal of letters and the flat perspective of his drawing, I also see the smiling faces and the ending affirmation, "You can." BJ also feels safe enough to label the page with the Arabic script he was learning from his father, a sign that the artists workshop was one of the positive aspects of BJ's school experience.

Billy, another student identified by our multidisciplinary team as learning disabled in language articulation and processing, found joy and self-esteem in his artistic expression (see Figure 3–7). "I am going to be an artist," he proudly proclaims. He shows his understanding of space, perspective, use of art materials, and a sophisticated understanding of written language in this page alone.

Conclusion

The artists workshop provides opportunities for children to express their rich use of written language: complex verb forms, descriptors, and specialized vocabulary. But it also provides much more. The workshop structure encourages flexible thinking, analysis, and change. Bringing more art materials into the classroom is fun for all of us and is a source of academic motivation for the children and for me. Through the process of sharing our artistic and literacy growth, we have created a new community bond as a classroom filled with people of diverse abilities and interests.

Jacob's perspective on art and his injunction, "Art is fun when you know what you are doing," keeps me mindful of my professional exploration of the connections between words and pictures, as well as of the simple pleasures of learning to be an artist and writer. Like Jacob, "I like art and creation. It is special to me."

References

Bjork, C. 1985. *Linnea in Monet's Garden.* New York: R and S Books.

Cummings, P. 1992. *Talking with Artists.* New York: Bradbury.

Ernst, K. 1994. *Picturing Learning.* Portsmouth, NH: Heinemann

Hubbard, R. 1993. "Time Will Tell." *Language Arts* 70(7):574–82.

Lionni, L. 1991. *Matthew's Dream.* New York: Alfred Knopf.

Venezia, M. 1988. *Rembrandt.* Chicago: Children's Press.

Warton, S. 1976. *Children's Crafts.* Menlo Park, CA: Lane.

4

Opening Up to Art:
Imagery and Story in a High School
Reading Class

Peter Thacker

Wague stood in front of our classroom admiring the illustrations of our many authors. He smiled. "We are all artists."

I looked up, "Yes, you see we can all be artists."

Wague calmly reiterated, "We are all artists."

I am a teacher first. I create assignments that I hope will push students to new creative and critical heights. I go to films and museums, read books, take part in discussions, always with a second me, my observer, in tow. Hmm, that Boll poem would be perfect for my junior class; I must recommend that my kids go to hear Gary Soto read; the HIV Day Center is a perfect place to send my students for community service.

I have considered myself at times to be a writer as well—of poetry and essays. But I have remained aloof from most writing in my classroom. I have to take roll; if I contact Grace's counselor, maybe I can keep her in school; I should talk to David—he's reading a book he won't enjoy.

I was not ready for the shock that propelled me to consider the possibility that I was an artist creating with my students rather than for them, or for the profound changes in my teaching occasioned by a short jaunt into the world of visual literacy.

Some Context

I work in an urban high school as a Chapter 1 reading teacher. The five classes I teach each day are made up of twelve to fifteen ninth- to twelfth-grade students. About two thirds of my students have English as their second language. Most are from Asian countries, but there are a few from Mexico, Russia, Rumania, Kenya. Almost all my students have not passed our district's graduation standard in reading—a standard an average fifth grader can pass.

This is not to say that my students aren't adequate readers; most can read many of the same books that other students in middle and high school read for pleasure. This discrepancy may come as a surprise. However, students will read with passion books that speak to them.

Take Alisia. She was in my reading program last year as a senior and came back this year as a tutor although she had not passed the reading test (she barely passed it this year). Alisia has always been an avid reader, particularly of books about wayward kids; she has been one, she knows. One weekend she took home *I, Juan de Pareja,* a Newbery winner about a slave and artist who became an assistant to the Spanish painter Velázquez. Alisia read it in one night and came back talking about how moved she was by Pareja's struggles.

Or take Larry, a boy who read almost nothing before coming to our program this year. He had been declared legally blind and his parents had used books on tape with him for years. In my initial testing, I found he was a slow but not terribly disabled reader. In one year, sometimes with help but often on his own, he read with comprehension and enthusiasm *Call of the Wild, Black Boy,* and *American Hunger* (Richard Wright's autobiographical sequel to *Black Boy*), and he is now reading Farley Mowat's *Never Cry Wolf.* He still hasn't passed the district reading test. Perhaps this has to do with the fact that the reading for the test seems distant, fragmented, and for someone else's purposes. It is stories that capture my students.

Genesis of a Project

My school's reading program uses tutors who work one-on-one with our students. Four days a week students work with mentors and on the fifth we do something as a group. The tutors come from a wide range of sources—retired teachers, community volunteers, and college practicum students, as well as peer tutors.

I wanted a way for my students and tutors to connect. English teachers know that students write narratives with greater fluency than exposition: story creates a sense of greater possibility, of involvement, of catharsis. Could telling the stories of others be a catalyst to better reading and writing? What if I had my students interview their tutors and produce stories from these oral histories?

I called my former dance teacher, Susan Banyas, who had done some work with oral histories in our school district as an artist-in-residence, and asked for her assistance. My coteacher Charlotte Pennington and I then wrote a proposal to the Teacher Incentive Program funded through a block grant from Title 2 funds. We got the grant and used the majority of the funds to bring artists into our classrooms to help our students solicit stories from their tutors and then retell these stories in their own way. And thus began a collaboration that challenged my notion of how to prepare students to write.

Images, Images, Images . . .

When I first conceived of this project, I did not view it as an exercise that incorporated visual imagery. I saw the project through my English teacher's lens: we'll interview, take notes, and write. I did not anticipate Susan's suggestion that we bring in a dancer, a storyteller-musician-potter, and a visual artist.

I was even more surprised when Susan began her first class by having students do stretches and then close their eyes while she guided them back to remembered images from their childhood. They then drew these images on three-by-five-inch cards, a close-up view of what Susan called interchangeably the "heart of the story" and the "central image." They wrote notes on the back of the cards, and then everyone began sharing these vignettes while their listeners were encouraged to identify the image they saw as central.

Sascha, an intern teacher, told this story:

My dad, my brother, and I went out boating on this pristine lake on which you could see the fish skimming through the water. My brother, who was about seven, got so excited that he went to the head of the boat to see a fish. He started to lean over and kept straining farther and farther to see that fish. One last lean and he fell into the water. He couldn't swim. My dad just reached out of the boat, caught him by his hair, and dragged him hair-first back into the boat.

We all wrote down images central to this story. Some students saw the boat, others saw the boy leaning over, others saw the fish, and some saw the boy's hair in the father's grip. All of the images were compact moments in time and all were central to the story.

Much of what we did to prepare students was visual. We watched *The Sewing Woman*, a filmed oral history of a Chinese woman who had emigrated to the United States. The pictures of wartime China, of cramped sewing rooms in San Francisco, of successful family members in their Sunday best, told a story as compelling as the words, sometimes spoken in Chinese, that swirled around them.

When Wague shared his stories from Mali, he first showed slides of Timbuktu and his village, then showed us fabric art and techniques for drawing and let us play instruments he himself had made. When I had spoken about Wague with Susan, she had identified him as a storyteller. Even though I knew him foremost as a potter, I didn't understand that imagery informed his stories.

Then there was Minh, telling us how he had developed his dance describing his flight from Vietnam. He used three central images: a handkerchief from his mother that he'd thrown away on the boat because he wanted to die and it was the only possession worth living for; rice spilling into the sea, because this act invites bad luck; and the ocean itself, a symbol of both separation and freedom. No images, no choreography.

Tom McKenna, another teacher schooled in oral history, came to help students with interviewing techniques and brought his films of black kids talking to Jewish older folks displaced by urban renewal. Images with words.

At the same time we were seeing others' work, we were creating our own: projects like "I am at," in which we closed our eyes and visualized six places, then fashioned little books of the visual images we'd seen, accompanied by a few words to explain them. The images were central and the words were reinforcement, often using the power of a repeated line, *I am at* or *I see,* to tie together disparate experiences in a poetic fashion. Images jumped from scenery to everyday experiences, each containing an intimated story much larger than the captured moment.

We told stories through photo montage. Susan introduced her grab bag of found materials, which ranged from wrapping paper to chicken wire to pieces of driftwood. Using a glue gun, watercolors, crayons, colored pencils, and collage techniques, we attacked the photos, creating visual stories, wordless except for maybe a caption or slogan. The photos took on a different cast as students tinted them or combined them or attached things to them. The stories became

FIGURE 4–1

distinctive, individual renderings. Sam's montage (Figure 4–1) used cut paper, a photo, netting, felt, hair bristles, fabric, and string to capture a humorous story of young love.

Learning from the Stories

I am an English teacher. I create images through words. I have kids touch the senses with words, but I don't use visual images to touch the words they use. What happens when the process becomes recursive, when images propel words and words compel images? It is here that the books about tutors become most instructive.

I am a speculator and I hope a good observer. These two characteristics have kept me fresh and excited as a teacher. However, I learned the hard way back in high school (thank you, Mr. Iverson) that if you have a "profound idea" in your mind, you'd better be able to find evidence in the text to back it up. And guess what? My opinions have this nasty habit of changing as I write my way in and out of them. Take the following then as informed speculation.

In the morning the nice lady made Hal a healthy breakfast.

The stories themselves were beautiful, heartwarming. They were distinctive not only because they were about individuals, but also because of the way the stories became the interviewers'. They were based on the stories told by the tutors, but the students created their own realities. For example, Cori's story of Bonnie falling from the swing somehow became a metaphor for family pain.

The stories tended for the most part to be short and direct. The endings demanded attention. They were funny or plaintive or dramatic or sometimes even profound. They had character. And they played off the illustrations.

FIGURE 4–2

Listen to Malcolm's beginning, "On a hot, greasy, and cheesy day, Rachel was slaving behind the black and only pizza stove," and ending, "As the ambulance left, poor old Rachel had to start back slaving behind that hot pizza stove."

Listen to Yarnell: "Robin's marriage was a love through a telephone. Everyone knows the phone is the best way."

Listen to Cori: "When she was on the branch she fell down on her back and all the air was pushed out of her body. She lay there thinking she must be dead. She lay there until she felt she could get up. She wasn't badly hurt. She still swings today though she wouldn't want to be a little girl again."

I believe the students' use of visual imagery helped them distill the essence of their stories, allowing them to use words compactly, carefully. There was such little use of unnecessary, general words. It is often the case in my classes that my students write without essentials, without the "guts" of their stories, as if the reader will fill in the context. Or they write in such generalities that it is hard to know what distinguishes their story from every other basketball or party or young love story. Not the case here. The essence of a moment in time was captured. Maybe it was the emphasis on a story *from* a life, not about a whole life, that directed the process. Maybe it was the photographs a particular interviewee brought to the interview. Maybe it was having someone available from whom to get details. Whatever it was, it worked.

Thoan interviewed Joni, who left the next day never to return. Joni's story was about a trip to Hawaii in which Joni and her boyfriend backpacked to "The Seven Waterfalls." Joni had brought photographs of the trip, but when Joni disappeared, Thoan was creating on his own. His piece was sparse—poetic in its sparseness. He began with Joni at home, and each page took his couple to a destination closer (Hawaii, the hotel, the rented car) to the waterfalls until they reached the "seven waterfalls" on the center page, the central image to which he built. Then for the last four pages he traced their return home. A picture per page, a story created through images, first visual, made concrete by a very few words.

In contrast, Donovan, in his story about Hal hitchhiking across the United

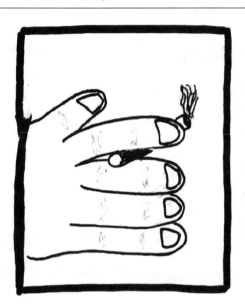

so Hal lit a cigarette and held it a half inch away from his fingers so when it burned 'em, Hal would start talking.

FIGURE 4–3

States during the Depression, located the heart of the story in words, then created images to reinforce the story. His images could not be fully understood without the story. For instance, one illustration was of a plate of eggs and bacon (Figure 4–2), another was of a hand holding a cigarette (Figure 4–3). The first image accompanies text that tells about a woman who fed and housed Hal for a night as he made his way to Oregon. The second accompanies text describing how Hal kept himself awake during a night as a passenger in a truck carrying explosives. In this situation, the story, the words, drove the images.

For many, visual images generated stories, then later the story suggested images. I think of Dong's description of how Steve's family cooked crawdads. When Steve first told his story, he brought a bunch of photos, some of which Dong photocopied and used to create photo montage. The pictures of family members stirring up the soup allowed him not only to describe the process but to give it humor, to create voice. The voice fed some visual humor. When telling about the spiciness of the food, Dong took a photo and added blue and brown yarn to the heads of two eaters, vividly portraying the shock of eating that stew (see Figure 4–4). Juxtapose this with the words: "But when the crawdads hit the newspaper, you'd better watch out 'cause the kids and parents are digging in." The spice is intimated; the delight is told.

FIGURE 4–4

Then there was Luba, recently emigrated from Russia via Italy, a seasoned traveler at the young age of fifteen. Her tutor Margueritte's story was also of traveling. Through illustration, Luba fuses her tutor's and her own life stories. On her first two pages Luba presents a photo of Margueritte now and an image of a young girl in a cart being pulled by a goat—the American and the European. On the next page is a map of Russia, along with the explanation that Margueritte has "to move to (sic) much because of [her father's] job" (see Figure 4–5). The words tell the story of the interviewer as well as the interviewee. Luba ends with the wonderful words, "Margueritte is not traveling physically as much these days but her reading takes her from place to place," illustrated by a train car that resembles a gypsy caravan. Two travelers bridge two cultures and three generations in a simple story brought to life by the illustrations.

The relationship between words and illustrations, then, can be recursive. A

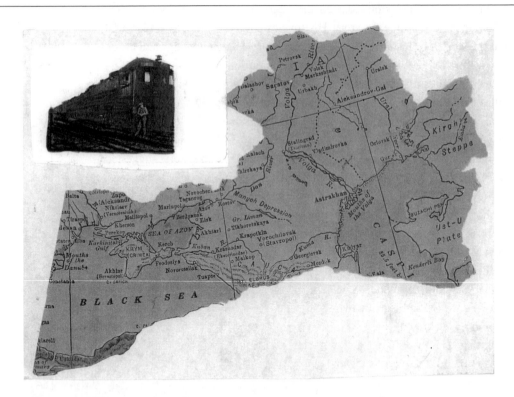

FIGURE 4–5

When Margueritte was little her father had a job and they had to move a lot. He did skilled larborer who installed sprinkler systems in lumber mills and warehouses whenever the Sprinkler Union sent him. So they had to move to much because of the job.

story propels an image, an image suggests words, these words may drive a new image. The stories are not strict recapitulations of the tutors' descriptions but a rich mix of visual and verbal imagery and of the tutors' and students' imaginations.

While several stories were lengthy, illustrations encouraged distillation. I don't want to claim that distillation is the only way to create a good story:

Dong's story was funny and informative in its complete elaboration. However, in my experience it is uncommon for Chapter 1 students to write clearly and concisely in their journals or other writing demanded of them in school. This was not the case here. The illustrations seemed to create a medium through which the essence of each story would shine and the extraneous could be excised. Eric described it this way as he explained what central image now meant to him: "You can get to the point without writing a lot."

The Teacher Changes

It is easy to lose the thread of personal changes brought about by this project. I have looked deeply at my students' work and described how they changed, how the project affected them. My students had fun. They explored visual images with gusto. They seemingly worried very little about how well they drew. They took the time to create words and images that were heartfelt and compelling. But what about the ways in which I changed?

My mom's family is filled with publishers. *Publisher's Weekly* recently did a short article on three generations of my family in the art-publishing business. Art books—Gaugin, Van Gogh, Picasso, Matisse—lived on my parents' coffee table throughout my childhood. I pored over them again and again—as an outsider. I knew the Fauvists and the German Expressionists and the Cubists. I saw their view of the world. I inhabited their emotions through color, texture, shape, and image. But it was a world from which I excluded myself. They were the creators. I was the consumer. I left art to the "artists." What a funny feeling to hear Wague say that we are all artists.

Here I am, the teacher turned artist. I have learned to inhabit my images. To encapsulate emotions, memories, even my subconscious in pictures. To find in the illustration the heart of the story. To let the words become the embellishment. I now write more with my students. I give them many more chances to use visual imagery to respond to writing, to explain feelings, ideas, stories. And I create those images myself.

5

Beyond Answers

Jill Ostrow

Six-year-old Kyle was about twenty minutes into drawing the "guys" in his picture to look exactly the way he was imagining them in his mind. I looked over his shoulder. His picture was typical for his artistic talent—precise, detailed, colorful—but he was using crayon, which was unusual; he usually drew with colored pencils. Although it was a wonderful piece of art, this wasn't art workshop; the kids were working on solving a mathematical problem.

"Kyle, this doesn't have to be a masterpiece, you know! I really love your drawing, but I'd like to see you try and solve the problem too, okay?" I felt terrible disturbing him like that, but I really wanted to see him solve the problem. "You can go back to the coloring after you have a solution. How's that?"

"Okay," he muttered. I watched as he got out of his chair, marched over to get a basket of Unifix cubes, and in seconds came up with a solution to the problem. The kids know that I always ask them to write how they solved problems, so Kyle wrote, "15. I GASH YOSD U NAFKS KOWBS." [15. I just used Unifix cubes.] He put the Unifix cubes back in the basket, marched them back to the shelf, and sat back down to continue his picture.

"So, how many people are you going to draw?" I asked him.

"Fifteen. Look at this guy flying with the balloons."

"That's cool. Kyle, before you used the Unifix cubes, how did you know how many people to draw?"

"Oh, I was counting after I did each person. But you wanted to see me solve it, and I wasn't done drawing, so that's why I got the Unifix cubes."

"Oh." What more could I say?

Over the years I have realized the importance of drawing as a way for children to solve mathematical problems, but it wasn't until I watched Kyle that I grasped all the connections. Kyle was able to use two strategies for solving problems—drawing and using manipulatives—just as many children do. And drawing is as valid a strategy as using manipulatives. If I hadn't questioned Kyle, I would have seen his picture simply as a piece of art, not as a problem he was trying to solve.

Kyle never did complete the drawing of the fifteen people. It took him two days to do four, and by then we were already on the next problem. But it was important for him not only to be able to draw as he did, but also to demonstrate that he could solve the problem.

I teach a class of first through third graders. The age range is four years, and the intellectual or academic range is even greater. In math workshop our class explores mathematical concepts—each child in ways that match her or his understanding. Just as I see every child at a different level of understanding during writing workshop, I see this difference during math workshop. Children learn to write by practicing and experimenting and exploring writing; children learn mathematical concepts the same way. Even if everyone is investigating the same concept, each child may have a very different experience.

The problems here are ones that I have written over the past couple of years. I don't get them from workbooks; I integrate them with what we are studying. One year, we became an island community, and our curriculum for the entire year grew out of that idea. The following year, we set up a time/travel chamber. Two of the places the kids chose to explore were 1863 (to learn about the Civil War) and the contemporary Arctic. Many of the problems discussed here relate to one or another of these topics.

In math workshop, kids also write their own problems, create their own math games, share what they are learning with one another, record what they are learning, take part in minilessons, and explore and investigate various concepts. I make spaces for children to move *beyond answers,* to understand concepts, to make explorations, and to investigate the mathematical process.

Understanding Concepts

Children use manipulatives not only to help them *solve* a problem, but also to help them *understand* the concepts inherent to a particular problem. Manipulatives are not the only vehicle for gaining understanding, however. Kyle, for instance, who is now a second grader in my class, often chooses pictures to help him solve problems. He has now learned to draw quick symbols to represent what he is trying to solve. In one problem, he was proving that three twenty-sixths of the class were wearing glasses. He started out by emphasizing the three children who wore glasses, drawing them in detail. He then went on to draw the remaining twenty-three members of the class as stick figures, thus showing his understanding of the concept of fraction (see Figure 5–1). Using manipulatives might have been more confusing for him.

Many younger children need to use their own drawings because that's the way they organize their thinking. Melissa, one of the youngest and most inexperienced problem solvers in my class, was working on a problem that

im Gowing to PRoV tHAt $\frac{3}{20}$ HAVe GIASSi's on in tHi's GLSS

CHuK AlissA tAsA

FIGURE 5–1

asked, *If there are 8 Union soldiers on a battlefield, how many legs would there be?* She drew eight stick figures, and then counted up the legs. I knew from her drawing that she could organize her thinking well enough to represent eight soldiers and count to sixteen. Another student solved the same problem by getting out two cubes eight times, showing me her beginning understanding of multiplication. Yet another child solved it by writing that $8 \times 2 = 16$, demonstrating her solid understanding of multiplication. It is important for me as a teacher to know that the concepts individual children use to approach a particular problem are often very different.

Division lends itself very nicely to pictorial representations. Jordan was solving a problem that required the concept of division:

A team of travelers is having a problem. They have 6 kayaks that hold 2 people each. But there are 13 people on the team. How many people will be able to travel in the kayaks? Will there be any extra? What should they do?

Drawing pictures as part of a story helped Jordon reach a solution, as his math work shows (see Figure 5–2).

Dave wrote a division problem based on his knowledge that a snowflake has six sides: *There are 34 sides. How many snowflakes? Are there any extra?* Carly solved Dave's problem by drawing thirty-four lines and then circling each group of six. I knew she had an understanding of division by her drawing; just seeing the answer would have been meaningless.

When children in my class *do* solve a problem in their heads and just write the answer, they know they will have to explain their thinking; that sometimes comes in the form of a picture. Morgan knew the answer to one problem very quickly. She wrote her explanation, and when I asked her to go back and show me what her thinking "looked like," she drew a picture and a chart (see Figure 5–3). She knew how to organize the problem in her head, she had a solid understanding of multiplication, and she could also show her thinking visually.

I have begun having the children create presentations for some of their solutions and share them with the whole class. These presentations serve two purposes. One, I am able to observe what the kids know about problem solving on a broader scale. They are not only solving the problem mathematically, they are also determining what materials to use, what will show up well in front of

FIGURE 5–2

an audience, and how they can explain the problem well enough so that the audience will understand the concepts they are trying to get across. Two, the visual nature of a presentation usually forces them to solve the problem in a different way, thus gaining further understanding of the concept.

Anna chose to present a problem that she had originally solved by using Unifix cubes:

> *There are 36 dogs on a team of dogsleds and 6 people. Each person needs to take a group of dogs. To make it fair, each person will take care of the same number of dogs. So, how many dogs will each person have to take care of?*

Her written explanation was, "There are 6 dogs in each group. I used cubes and put them into groups." Her presentation was much more detailed. She cut out six people and glued them onto a piece of poster board. She then cut out thirty-six dogs and divided them evenly between each cutout person. It was clear that she understood what she had done: "Well, first I cut out these people.

FIGURE 5–3

Those are the ones that need to take care of the dogs. Then, I cut out these dogs. Thirty-six of them. Then, I said to myself, One for you, one for you, one for you all the way 'til there wasn't any more left." When she was finished, the audience offered comments or asked questions. Many students commented about how easy it was to understand the picture, saying that is was neat and her explanation was clear.

Carly and Tessia worked together on their presentation for this problem:

11 hunters each killed 2 seals. Then, they put all of their seals in a pile and divided them up equally among 6 families. How many seals would each family get? Will their be extra? How many extra? What should the hunters do with the extra?

The display for their presentation was great. They used black poster board for the background and bright colors for the pictures. They made the eleven hunters out of green paper and put two orange circles representing the seals next to the hunters. Then they drew six families and showed that each family would get three and there would be four extra seals. They also made a key explaining their symbols. They presented the problem together, and each had a different idea about what would happen to the extra seals.

Tessia: "I thought that they could split the seals in half and then each family could get another half, and then the extra seal could go to the dogs."

Carly: "I thought that they could use the seals for clothes and stuff like that."

Transitions and Strategies

Children often go through stages, first using pictures to help them solve problems, then using more abstract symbols. Chris made the transition from picture to symbol in the middle of a problem. The problem was:

One time/travel chamber has 2 doors and 5 windows. How many doors and windows would 2 chambers have?
    4 chambers?
    5 chambers?
    10 chambers?

Chris began his solution by drawing actual chambers with doors and windows, then counting up all the doors and windows. When he got to five chambers, his drawing was less detailed, and by the time he got to ten chambers, he had figured out that he just needed to write the number instead of drawing all the windows and doors (see Figure 5–4). He also showed his knowledge of grouping numbers. Instead of counting by ones, he knew to group the numbers by fives and twos to solve the problem more efficiently.

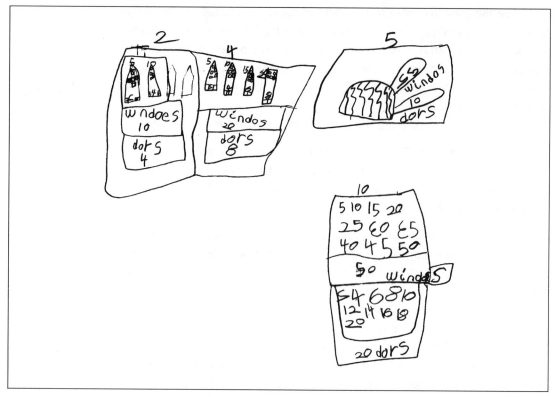

FIGURE 5–4

It is wonderful to see a transition like that from one child in one problem, but it is also interesting to observe different children solving the same problem and how each uses pictures and drawing differently. Several children used drawings in connection with the following problem, yet the ways in which they used the pictures were very different.

> *It takes 2 hours to cut down one small palm tree. How long would it take to cut down 2 small palm trees and 4 large palm trees if the large palm trees are 4 times as big as the small ones?*

Torin first drew a picture of the palm trees. He drew two trees and then four larger trees, but couldn't figure out how to get an answer by just using his picture. He had seen some other kids using graph paper and figured out that if the small palm trees were two squares, then the large ones would be eight. He drew a rectangle on the graph paper that was eight squares, counted that four times, and then added four. His original picture was no use to him for solving this problem; however, he did draw four of the trees bigger than the first two.

Kyle used graph paper to draw his trees. He wrote, "First I made two palm trees then I made four big palm trees. I pretended the little palm tree was hooked together with the big palm trees and I did that four times. It would take

36 hours." By looking at Kyle's pictures and his written explanation (see Figure 5–5), I saw how he had made the big palm trees four times as large as the small ones. He then got thirty-six by counting all of the squares in his trees. For this particular problem, pictures were Kyle's way of organizing his thinking.

JB also used graph paper as a way of grouping by twos. He wrote the numbers by twos as he was counting and stopped when he came to the end of his two-square groupings.

Laura's drawings didn't look like an aid to her in terms of counting to solve the problem. Instead of drawing trees in two-square units, which would be the logical way for solving the problem using drawings, Laura drew them in three-square units, showing me that she was using the drawings only as a way of seeing the size difference. Her explanation was done with numbers.

Tessia solved the problem in her head, wrote how she solved the problem, and *then* drew pictures to show the size difference. Her drawings were not part of how she solved the problem either.

FIGURE 5–5

This shows me not just how many different strategies children use to solve problems, but how many different *picture* strategies they use. Children need to be able to use many strategies—and combinations of strategies—for solving problems. Some children, like Kyle, use a combination of words and pictures. Other children use a combination of pictures and manipulatives, as Anna did in her problem about the dogs. And some children use a combination of all three as a strategy for solving problems as Carly did for the following problem:

10 palm trees grew out of the ground. 5 of them each grew 6 coconuts. The other 5 grew 3 coconuts. Then a monkey came along and took away 13 of the coconuts. How many coconuts were left? How did you get your answer?

Carly organized her thinking by using drawings and symbols to show the number of coconuts on each tree. She used arrows to show how many were taken away by the monkey. Then she went to get cubes to check her work and came up with the same answer. Her written explanation clearly describes her thinking: "½ had six coconuts and the other ½ had three coconuts. The coconuts add up to 45 so $45 - 13 = 32$." She solved this problem using three different strategies: first, she drew a pictorial representation of her thinking; then, she checked what she had done by manipulating cubes; and finally, she wrote an algorithm for how she had solved the problem using numbers. All of the children in my class can make any or all of these choices in solving problems.

Explorations

During math workshop, the kids also have an opportunity to create their own learning situations. They create games, write their own problems, and explore and investigate new concepts. Sometimes I structure the investigations. For example, one day I asked the kids to explain a specific number. That was the only instruction I gave, to explain the number given. Paige was to explain the number 12. She drew a picture of her hands and then two more fingers. She told me that she knew she had ten fingers, so she drew those and then had to draw two more to make twelve. Carly needed to explain the number 875. First, she drew a picture that told a story—a stick figure walking a dog—and wrote 600 next to the dog and 100 next to the person. She then drew a tree next to the person and wrote 100 next to the tree. Next to the tree, she drew a cloud and wrote 75. She was not only exploring the number I had given her, but trying to fit the number into a story. She also showed 875 using place value strips; she showed what $8.75 looked like; and she wrote that 875 was an odd number.

Explorations such as these let children challenge themselves. There is no right or wrong answer; they are simply investigations.

In another investigation I asked the kids how they could see and write fractions using Pattern Blocks. Dave investigated the blocks by writing everything he could about each one: "½ of a yellow is a red. It takes 6 greens to fill in a yellow. 1 green is ⅙ of a yellow. 3 greens make a red and that is half of a yellow." Kyle challenged himself by giving a value to the blocks. He drew the red trapezoid and gave it a value of 1. He drew the yellow hexagon, and knew that if the red was 1, the yellow had to be 2. He figured out that the green triangle was ⅓ and the blue diamond was ⅔. Then Kyle drew pictures connecting the blocks. First he drew a hexagon with a triangle on top of it and figured out the value of that drawing would be 2⅓. He then created several more drawings, determining the value of each based on the original value he had given the red block.

Some investigations take the form of more open-ended projects. When someone at a conference asked me, "Since you don't do worksheets, how do you know your kids know their math facts?" I decided to pose that question to my students and challenge them to create a drawing or some other representation that would show me. Carly proved she knew her two-times tables by building a tower out of paper cubes, adding two cubes at a time. Dave drew an elaborate Civil War battlefield that showed he knew how to multiply by four: the group of soldiers kept increasing by four. Kiersten proved she could add to ten by drawing a huge picture of Unifix cube towers. These representations showed me my kids not only *knew* their math facts, they also *understood* the facts well enough to explain them. Just knowing the answer to a problem is not enough; understanding the *process* is a far more vital outcome. Being able to show some sort of representation, be it drawings, pictures, or words, is crucial to a child's mathematical development.

Process

Using pictures, drawings, and manipulatives is not necessarily related to age development. I teach a class of children ranging in ages from six to nine and there is a wide variety of ways in which the children use aids to help them solve problems. First grader Jacob rarely uses manipulatives, whereas Grant, a third grader, always does. Kyle, a second grader, always uses pictures; Kiersten, a second grader, always uses manipulatives; and Megan, a second grader, usually relies on words and symbols. Many adults I know count on their fingers, others use calculators, still others can solve problems quickly in their heads. Children need the opportunity to use a variety of strategies to develop their own process for approaching problem solving.

As an adult, I am just now learning how to look at mathematical concepts visually. I was taught to memorize facts and algorithms. Now I solve the same problems my children do by using drawings, or I explain my thinking by using pictures. I am definitely a visual thinker. Because I was not allowed to learn that way, I assumed I was just "bad" at math. As it turns out, I've discovered that I am a pretty competent mathematician; I just needed to use a process that was right for me. I hope I am giving my students the same opportunity to discover their own process for organizing and explaining their thinking and understanding the concepts they need to learn.

6

Putting Art
on the Scientist's Palette

Mary Stein and Brenda Power

We are sisters—a scientist (Mary) and a writer (Brenda). These labels help define us, but they do not necessarily describe who we are or how we view the world. The scientist writes and the writer does science, and we both rely on words and images in our work. Thinking of ourselves as Renaissance women, with many talents and interests, is not only less constraining but helps us reach beyond our labeled domain.

We've heard high school and college students proclaim, "I've always been a math and science person," or, "I have the heart and perspective of an artist; science has never been my strong point," buying into the notion that one can be either a scientist or an artist but not both. Before some students have finished adolescence, they have narrowly defined who they are by labeling their perceived strengths.

New workshop approaches to teaching help students avoid narrow definitions of their strengths as thinkers and learners. Writing is one of the best tools students have to expand their view of the roles of artists and scientists. As students write about scientific concepts, they often move easily between words and images. By looking at how students try to interpret and understand concepts through writing, we find ways to integrate science and art in the classroom.

The leap past narrow definitions of student abilities begins with the dissolving of boundaries between disciplines. During the Renaissance, artists were scientists and scientists were artists. The close relationship between art and science is still obvious to the artist and to the scientist. In her account of patterns of creative thought, Vera John-Steiner describes the lives and experiences of talented and accomplished scientists. She concludes that productive thought doesn't follow a uniform pattern:

Curiosity and passion are maintained and renewed in the course of a scientist's career through the pleasures of discovery and through the use of varied kinds of thought when confronted with new and intriguing problems. Some scientists identify visual processes as crucial to their thinking, while others emphasize metaphoric or mathematical processes. (p. 173)

John-Steiner provides many examples illustrating the connection between the arts and the sciences as creative pursuits. For some, the ability first to visualize a solution and then to create a record of this vision through writing, experimenting, verbalizing, or drawing is the essence of creativity and discovery. Or, as Ewens (1989) states, "Our reflective activities enable us to uncover what is given, to unveil it, to reveal it, to render it explicit in words, artworks, rituals, sciences, religions, and the other embodiments of human meaning."

Adult Learners Versus Young Children

This ideal portrait of the purposes and forms of reflection is sadly missing when you examine the work of most adult learners. As we studied the science journals of preservice elementary teachers who were students in a physical science course, we noticed that few, if any, used drawings of any type. This surprised us. We think of drawings and visual representations as another language whereby people describe and understand their world. Language has been described as a mechanism for solving problems: "People use language as a tool to direct their intellectual power to problems in much the same way people use tools to direct their physical power to problems" (Greenfield 1991).

If artwork is yet another tool that students might use from a well-stocked language toolkit, then why weren't students using this tool when it seemed to best match the demands of scientific problems? These same students often use visual representations and various types of creative artwork in other areas of their lives, such as creating portfolios, bulletin boards, and projects. What is it that hinders the use of visual representations during scientific studies?

We asked these students to take home a pair of Rainbow Glasses and look through them at light from three different sources. These glasses separate light into all the colors of the spectrum and yield a dramatic array of colors. Scientifically, the glasses demonstrate that white light comprises all the colors of the spectrum. Visually, the effect is strikingly beautiful. We were curious how students would record their observations and very surprised when only two of twenty-six students drew pictures of what they had observed. Most wrote paragraphs describing what they saw, like Connie's, for example:

The candle had eight other candles reflected around it and each candle had one ray coming out from the tip of the candle flame. The flame was blue, green, yellow, and red. There was a well-defined boundary between each color and each color seemed to be of equal length.

As we read these descriptions we thought, wouldn't it have been easier and perhaps more accurate simply to draw what was observed? The two students who drew visual representations of their observations (see Figures 6–1 and 6–2) felt obliged to explain why they thought it was appropriate. Heather wrote, "Looking through my 'Science Glasses,' I though that it was better to draw what I saw than trying to write it." Similarly, after describing her observations in writing, Amber directed us to her drawings: "Look at the sketches to better understand what I saw."

Young children offer a stark contrast. In Jane Doan and Penny Chase's multiage K–2 classroom, a different child is the student observer each morning while the whole group sits and reads a message composed by the teachers. The student observer sits to the side of the group with one of the teachers. Working independently, both the teacher and child make notes on Post-Its of what they notice. At the end of the morning message session, both the teacher and child who have been observing tell the whole group what they have written down.

The children's sense of what language and visual tools might be used in this activity is very broad. Five-year-olds are often much more comfortable using visual representations. Sarah observes that Michael often raises his hand, and she notes her observation with this image, showing a hand and half circles on either side to represent gestures of waving:

First grader Aaron's drawing of the message board, with a much larger pair of eyes about it, is his way of showing that Bridget paid attention:

Jake shows Sarah was a good listener through a set of vibrating ears:

Most children capture between six and twelve observations on Post-Its when it is their turn to be the student observer. These are all saved in notebooks, and throughout the year the whole class is able to determine patterns for individual students and the entire group. This daily activity helps the children gain the fundamental skills of observation, looking for patterns, and drawing conclusions about a classmate's behavior and learning.

SCE ~~520~~ 502
Dr. Mary Stein
October 10, 1994

$\frac{10}{10}$ Good Observators

Looking through my "Science Glasses," I thought that it was
better to draw what I saw rather than trying to write it.

1) 60 Watt bulb:
Working from nearer to the light source to farer, I saw the following
colors in this order:

indigo
blue
green
yellow
orange
red

8 distinct groups

2) Light blue neon bulb in the follow shape ⌐

CCC
CCC
CCC

Same color pattern as above
yellow was much more defined

8 distinct groups
(lighter colors- more pastel)

3) Match

Same color pattern as above
8 distinct groups

FIGURE 6-1

Excellent Report 10/10

Amber
SCE 502
Oct. 10, 1994

Experimenting with Rainbow Glasses

I put on my glasses while sitting at my desk while the light was on. As I glanced around the room, I noticed that the little orange indicator light on my light switch was reflecting only three colors (yellow, orange, red). I looked at my red digital clock and it only reflected one color (red). So I decided to look at it in the dark and draw what it looked like.

Then I lit a candle. I looked at it the dark. I thought that this was the prettiest of all the light sources I looked at. It had a prominent pattern of eight colored lines containing all the lights of the rainbow (violet, blue, green, yellow, orange, red); then there were several lighter and narrower lines extending further from the candle.

Another light I thought was interesting was the street light. It had a similar pattern to the candle except that it also reflected the light bulb (a round shape) in a peculiar way. The "bulbs" were not symmetrical. The most prominent colors were the blue, green, orange, and red with a long space between the blue and green and the others clumped together.

(Look at the sketches to better understand what I saw)

FIGURE 6–2

Some teachers might argue that the student observer activity isn't "science" at all, again illustrating how narrowly we have defined science to include only activities that move in a lockstep way toward understanding a metered-out portion of conceptual knowledge. In reality, the process of the children in this multiage classroom closely mirrors the complexity of the daily life of scientists in all disciplines, who must view a vast array of data, consider innumerable possibilities, consult with colleagues, and then make choices to discern patterns.

Mary Stein &
Brenda Power

Reform Theory Versus Current Practice

Reform efforts in science education emphasize that students need to construct scientific understanding through hands-on activities, collaboration, articulation, and reflection. These same goals are echoed in almost every subject area. In reading and writing, as in science, students need to be taught how to ask relevant questions, make predictions, acquire information from many sources, weigh alternatives, and reach defensible explanations. In science, as in other subject areas, the emphasis is on thinking and communicating:

> *Although understanding a few key concepts is important, the real challenge is teaching children how to do, think, read, and write about science. Like reading and writing, science is a dynamic process in which students must be actively involved constructing and revising understanding. Central to doing and learning science are observing and interacting with real world objects and events, making predictions about how they work, reading to research what others have learned about them, and constructing and writing explanations. (Reif & Larkin 1991)*

Contrasting the visual representations of Jane Doan and Penny Chase's young students as they record their observations and collect data on their classmates with the work of famous scientists and artists seems natural. Just as Andy used a picture of a big mouth to represent a lot of talking, Michelangelo incorporated his knowledge of human anatomy into his "Creation of Adam" fresco on the ceiling of the Sistine Chapel in the Vatican. For hundreds of years, the interpretation of this masterpiece was that God is passing the spark of life to Adam. An alternative interpretation, through a scientific lens, yields a different explanation (Meschberger 1990). In the fresco, God is shown against a dark background that resembles an outline of the human brain, including lateral cerebral fissure, cranium, spinal cord, and pituitary stalk. Michelangelo may have used his scientific knowledge of human anatomy to suggest that Adam's real gift from God was not life but intellect.

The work of young children and prominent scientists indicates that using visual language is a natural part of science. Yet as students get older, they rely less and less on visual tools and more on verbal tools. There are two possible reasons.

First, as children learn to read and write, part of the process involves becoming more comfortable with written communication. They may simply forget about using the visual tools they relied on earlier in their lives. Also, many teachers are uncomfortable with using images to convey meaning. It sends a powerful message to young children when they are no longer allowed to draw pictures during writing time or when paper for science logs is fully lined, with no white space for drawing. This message is often conveyed to children by the end of first grade in many schools.

Second, using visual representations and art to generate scientific understanding is not often emphasized or encouraged in connection with scientific methods. Most textbooks describe the scientific method as a linear process: identifying the problem, observing, hypothesizing, collecting data, reaching conclusions, and communicating results. This method does not address the visualization process that John-Steiner describes in her studies of the scientific mind. Nor does this description suggest that there are many possible routes to scientific discovery. As Mullis and Jenkins (1988) state, "In spite of what is sometimes reported about scientific investigations, especially in secondary school science textbooks, inquiry is often idiosyncratic. Furthermore, there is no 'scientific method.' *The notion that there is a scientific method should be dispelled from science teaching*" (p. 46, italics in original).

Reforms in science education have emphasized a "hands-on, minds-on" approach. Although the primary emphasis has been on encouraging the "doing of science through hands-on investigations," teachers are now beginning to focus on communication. In a special issue of the *Journal of Research in Science Teaching* devoted to reading and writing in science, many authors stress the importance of language and visualization to help students learn science concepts (Holliday, Yore & Alvermann 1994). The message to teachers was that hands-on science, alone, is not enough. Similarly, teachers may be neglecting a particularly useful learning tool in their art curriculum. As one art educator has stated, "Scientific illustration is a broad area that has been neglected, particularly in the secondary schools" (Gainer & Child 1986).

Visualization and Drawing in Secondary Classrooms

Some examples of how visualization and drawing are used in school classrooms demonstrate how fostering drawing and artwork may help promote student understanding. One seventh-grade teacher who had been trying to help his students understand simple machines challenged them to design a complex machine to do a daily chore. When asked how he came up with the idea for his milk-pouring machine (see Figure 6–3), John explained, "I wanted to draw something that had a lot of different parts. I wanted it to work." A close look at the machine reveals how drawing helped this student think more

FIGURE 6–3

deeply about his understanding of related scientific concepts. The designs this teacher's students drew were creative, inventive, and incorporated the scientific principles they had been taught.

Still, when asked to visualize and draw their thoughts on paper, many older students are confounded. At the beginning of the school year, a teacher in a high school science classroom asked his students to draw what they would see if they were looking at water through a superpowerful microscope. He wanted to find out how good they were at visualization and what they knew about water molecules. Some of the students became confused or frustrated, perhaps viewing the task as "busy work" and "nonscientific."

As students learned more about water, however, their visual representations began to reflect their scientific understanding. They were able to make spatial representations of the hydrogen and oxygen atoms that make up water molecules. From the drawings, the teacher gleaned a great deal of information about student understanding of and misconceptions about water and molecules not available in their written descriptions. Drawing representations of scientific phenomena forces students to think about the details of their visualizations.

Science, Art, and Language

Using writing and drawing to conceptualize ideas is not common in many high school classrooms. Even traditional forms of scientific writing, like lab reports and notebooks, are not commonly integrated with instruction. In the science section of the 1986 National Assessment of Educational Progress, nearly half of all Grade 11 students participating reported never writing lab reports (41 percent) or written reports of any kind (52 percent) (Mullis & Jenkins 1988). In many high schools, subject areas are segregated and there is little communication or collaboration among teachers in different disciplines. Students write in English class, use the scientific method in science class, and do artwork only if they have selected art as an elective.

Rather than thinking about science, art, and language as separate areas on a continuum, it is time to think about the similarities. In 1923, Robert Henri wrote, "When the artist is alive in any person, whatever his kind of work may be, he becomes an inventive, searching, daring, self-expressive creature. . . Where those who are not artists are trying to close the book, he opens it and shows there are still more pages possible." Replacing the word *artist* in Henri's description with *scientist* or *writer* creates a valid description of these labels as well. The description is one of a creative learner—someone who uses a multitude of talents, skills, knowledge, and resources to understand and explain the world.

There are many practical things educators at all levels can do to encourage the integration of science, art, and language. Like Doan and Chase, they can look at the areas of their curriculum where observation and note taking play an important role. A student observation activity like the one incorporated into their morning message time is not an add-on. It gives students an opportunity to demonstrate their individual "multitude of talents," systematically compiling information about the class.

Throughout the day, the tools of science and art can be made available in addition to that of language. When students can choose the kinds of papers and materials they will use in writers workshop, they are more likely to continue to make meaning through images. They need both blank and lined paper and many different kinds of writing instruments.

Science logs need to be constructed in a way that allows different representations of information. Imagine the difference between the representations of molecules in water when students are told to use lined paper and pens and when they can also use watercolors, pastel crayons, and easels.

Teachers need to move away from the narrow curricular boundaries that define the school day and often inhibit connections between disciplines. Many works of art, like Michelangelo's drawing, can be viewed through the lens of both artist and scientist. There are books and CD-ROMs that show the sketches and artistic renderings that led to important scientific discoveries. A case study of one Renaissance figure like Leonardo would show students how the tools of communication and making meaning dissolve the boundaries of art and science.

As more educators come to view learning as a holistic process in which students should be encouraged to use a wide variety of learning tools and processes, we may begin to return to the age of Renaissance—an age when artists were scientists and scientists were artists and language in its many forms linked them all.

References

Collette, A., and E. Chiapetta. 1994. *Science Instruction in the Middle and Secondary Schools.* New York: Macmillan.

Ewens, T. 1989. "Discipline: Science and Art as Reflective Activities." *Design for Arts in Education* 90(4):2–14.

Gainer, R. S., and J. S. Child. 1986. "Scientific Illustration for the Elementary School." *Art Education* 39(6):19–22.

Greenfield, P. M. 1991. "Language Tools and the Brain." *Behavioral and Brain Sciences* 14:531–95.

Holliday, W. G., L. D. Yore, and D. E. Alvermann. 1994. "The Reading-Science Learning-Writing Connection: Breakthroughs, Barriers and Promises." *Journal of Research in Science Teaching* 31(9):877–93.

John-Steiner, V. 1985. *Notebooks of the Mind: Explorations of Thinking.* Albuquerque, NM: University of New Mexico Press.

Meschberger, F. L. 1990. "An Interpretation of Michelangelo's Creation Based Upon Neuroanatomy." *Journal of the American Medical Association* 264(14):1837–41.

Mullis, I. V. S. and L. B. Jenkins. 1988. *The Science Report Card: Elements of Risk and Recovery.* Trends and achievement based on the 1986 National Assessment of Educational Progress. Princeton, NJ: Educational Testing Service.

Reif, F., and J. H. Larkin. 1991. "Cognition in Scientific and Everyday Domains: Comparison and Learning Implications." *Journal of Research in Science Teaching* 28:733–60.

7

Imagination Through Images: Visual Responses to Literature

Ruth Shagoury Hubbard

I couldn't read without forming a visual image. I've never read any fiction so abstract that you wouldn't form a visual image. I've never read a fiction that doesn't have a landscape, doesn't create a world, some kind of space. And we can see what's in it.

—John Hawkes

In a series of interviews with the authors John Hawkes, William Gass, and Carlos Fuentes, Ellen Esrock (1986) found that in explaining their reading experiences they frequently mentioned the importance of images. She concludes that the mental experiences of readers are complex, rich, and filled with images, which in turn encourage deeper connections to literature.

This conclusion does not apply only to adults. My interviews with and observations of younger readers also highlight the importance mental pictures have in bringing stories to life. As children respond to the words on the page by calling up familiar images or imagining new ones, they forge a stronger connection with literature and also understand the texts they read at a deeper level.

As we share literature with children and adolescents, we want to foster their genuine reactions and responses—and we want to find ways to link their own experiences to the ones in the books they read. Recent literary theory stresses that the best way to help students understand books is to encourage them to make those personal connections (Rosenblatt 1982).[1] In order to help our students become better readers, we need to help them read more intelligently and perceptively—to see what the works they read teach them about themselves and about the text itself.

---

[1] *In what has been termed a "reader response" approach to literature, teachers establish a classroom climate that encourages readers to actively engage with the text, drawing on their background experiences in order to construct meaning. For more information on this approach, both its theoretical foundation and practical application, see Karolides (1992) and Purves et al. (1995).*

Fortunately, current trends in literacy instruction are taking seriously the notion that children need to use their minds flexibly, take creative leaps in their thinking, and take the initiative in their learning strategies. Just as more teachers are welcoming visual literacy into their writing programs (as several chapters in this volume attest), we are also inviting visual responses into reading workshops and literature programs.

By including visual responses to literature, we can tap into areas that we might not reach through talking or writing. In a compelling chapter entitled "Making the Reading Visible," Alan Purves, Theresa Rogers, and Anna Soter (1995) eloquently express the possibilities:

> Visual responses can have [the] function of unlocking thoughts and feelings in response to literature, enabling us to stand back from the work itself and develop a sense of what we have not yet seen or an angle we have not previously considered. At the same time, visual response permits us to express with dignity what we feel and think. Our response does not have to die before it ever emerges. (p. 149)

For the past several years, I have been a coresearcher with two teacher-researchers in rural Oregon, investigating young children's mental processes as they learn to read, write, and problem solve. During the 1989–1991 school years, I was a member of Nancy Winterbourne's second-grade class in Molalla for one or two mornings per week. Nancy and I learned a great deal about how children use art and writing in their thinking processes (Hubbard 1993; Winterbourne, this volume). Since the fall of 1992, I have spent one full day per week in Jill Ostrow's multiage classroom (children ages six through nine years old) in Wilsonville, exploring children's creative development within classroom structures that value their abilities and build curriculum around their needs and interests (Hubbard 1996; Ostrow 1995). In both classrooms, the key role of memory images in the meaning-making process became apparent. The children themselves have been the essential informants.

Second Graders Show the Way

By looking carefully at the children's work and through interviews with them, Nancy and I began to see how important memory images are in their reading and writing processes. One of my favorite examples is from Amy's writing journal from the winter of 1990. One morning after Nancy had read aloud *A River Dream* (Say 1988), Amy reflected on her mental process (see Figure 7–1). As the story unfolded, Amy created memory images in her mind of the times she had been fishing with her family, and she was able to re-create this process on paper. She ended by paying compliments to the story itself, with a little window that opens to reveal the word *nice*.

Kathryn, for another example, wrote about the Miss Nelson books, touching on a range of memories, from Halloween to the mental image of the principal in the book dressed as a woman:

I like Halloween. It's fun, especially when you get candy. I love candy. And I like to dress up for Halloween. I'm going to write about Miss Nelson books. They are neat. Miss Viola Swamp is mean. I'd hate to have Miss Viola Swamp for a substitute. She'd be mean and it wouldn't be too much fun to have all that homework. I hope I never have Viola Swamp for a substitute and I hope I never have her as a coach. I wouldn't want to do all those leg warm-ups and run that fast. And I like when Mr. B comes out on the field and he's dressed up like a girl. He's funny.

We found that even less sophisticated readers were far more likely to choose to write about their books—and to talk about how much they enjoyed them—when they made connections between what they read and their own life experiences.

As we reread the children's journals and focused on the entries of the students who spontaneously drew and wrote about memory images in relation to their reading, we were struck by their involvement. Across a range of

FIGURE 7–1

abilities, the children talked about *enjoying* the experience of conjuring up and reliving their mental images. When children made that deeper personal connection to the stories they read, they were much more engaged in the book and enjoyed the reading experience. This is turn sparked their interest in reading more, expanding their experiences and giving them the practice that helped them become more fluent readers.

Based on these initial findings, Nancy decided to try a kind of visual response log in which students could connect their personal experiences to what they read. Work with these visual response logs didn't replace their regular literature journals and didn't take place daily—or even weekly—but the children were periodically asked to pick a book and draw and write two kinds of responses:

- Their favorite section of the book.
- What was going on in their mind as they read or heard the story.

Responding to books in words and pictures opened up new meanings and new connections for the children, inviting them all—regardless of their differences—to participate. Nancy first tried this with *Charlie and the Chocolate Factory* (Dahl 1977). Jenny loved the part in the book where the elevator went soaring through the house. It reminded her of the feeling in her stomach when she jumped on a trampoline (see Figure 7–2). Candace, on the other hand, was reminded of experiences with her sister. In her visual response, we see her sister's huge mouth screaming, "I want a candy bar," while Candace crunches away on her chocolate in the corner, replying, "Forget it" (see Figure 7–3).

As the children shared their writing and drawing, they thought of new anecdotes and memories, deepening their connections to different parts of the stories. Because of the success of this initial experience, Nancy made it a regular component of her reading workshop. We found that this format, while offering a range of choices—choice of book, choice of what to draw and write about—also provides a structure that *nudges* kids to make the kinds of connections that can help them become more involved in the reading experience.

The children made many important connections to the stories they read, teaching us and each other about the ways experiences enter their reading world. Here are the major categories we found in the children's responses:

- Memories of experiences similar to those in the book.
  Starla, for example, read a book about best friends and was reminded of her friendship with Lacey, her "best best friend"; Kevin was reminded of playing pirates with his friends when he read about children's experiences with pirates.

Your Name ___JeNNY___

Title of the Book ___Charlic, and, The, Chocolate, facTc___

Today's Date _____

- -

Draw a picture of your favorite part of the book.

Write one or two sentences explaining your drawing.

I LIKe weN The eLUVaT weNT IN The HOUSe

- -

Draw a picture of what happens in your thoughts when you think
about this book. What does it remind you of?

Write one or two sentences to explain your ideas.

iT REMiNS MY OF weN I JUMT
ON a chapLeN

FIGURE 7–2

Your Name ___Candice___

Title of the Book ___Charlie and the Choclate factory___

Today's Date ___December 19, 1989___

- -

Draw a picture of your favorite part of the book.

Write one or two sentences explaining your drawing.

when they ca flying out of the roof

- -

Draw a picture of what happens in your thoughts when you think about this book. What does it remind you of?

Write one or two sentences to explain your ideas.

Forget it,

Crunch crunch

I want a candy bar!

It reminds me of when I buy a cand bar with my al ou and my sister

FIGURE 7-3

Your Name _Kathryn_

Title of the Book _Saint George and The Drag_

Today's Date _April 26, 1991_

****

Draw a picture of your favorite part of the book.

Write one or two sentences explaining your drawing.

The Red Cross stoped the Dragon knight

Draw a picture of what happens in your thoughts when you think
about this book. What does it remind you of?

Write one or two sentences to explain your ideas.

it reminds me about the paper bag Prinssess cause of the dragon but the Prinssess rosccos the Prince

FIGURE 7–4

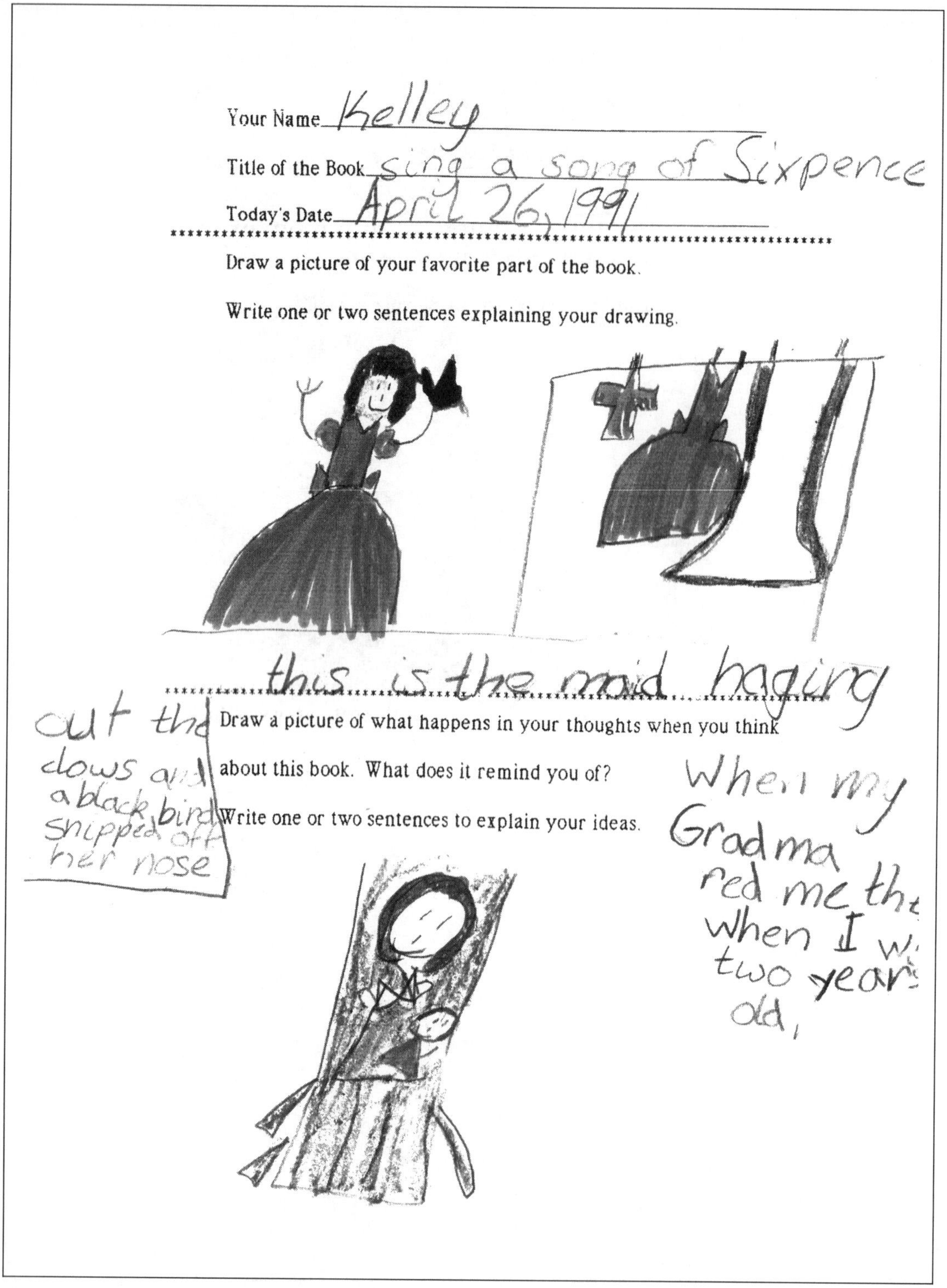

Your Name _Kelley_

Title of the Book _sing a song of Sixpence_

Today's Date _April 26, 1991_

∗∗∗

Draw a picture of your favorite part of the book.

Write one or two sentences explaining your drawing.

∗∗∗∗∗∗∗∗∗∗∗∗∗∗∗∗∗∗∗∗∗ _this is the maid haging_

out the   Draw a picture of what happens in your thoughts when you think
clows and   about this book. What does it remind you of?
a black bird
snipped off   Write one or two sentences to explain your ideas.
her nose

When my
Grandma
red me the
when I w.
two years
old,

FIGURE 7–5

- Memory images of particular details.

    In some cases, the pictures that came to mind caused kids to imagine particular details of the book more clearly. When Shellie read *Grandfather Twilight* (Berger 1984) (in which Grandfather Twilight creates a necklace in the sky), for example, she was reminded of a pearl necklace she had seen. When Travis read *The Book of Foolish Machines* (Pape 1988), he graphically described the "sqwushed bugs" he had tucked away in his bag of memories.

- Memory images of other books.

    Drawing on their memories of other stories, the children often compared and contrasted elements from them. In Kathryn's response to *Saint George and the Dragon* (Hodges 1984), she noted how the role of the princess differed from that of the heroine in *The Paper Bag Princess* (see Figure 7–4).

- Sensory images.

    The "unpleasant voice" in *Miss Nelson Is Missing* (Allard & Marshall 1977) recalled for Peter his sister's "mean voice." We found several examples of this kind of sensory memory image—voices, smells, or tactile sensations that forged deeper connections to the stories.

- Memories of people they know.

    Many times, the children wrote about or drew characters in the books as looking like family members or other people they knew. In the discussions that followed the sharing of visual responses like this, we would often hear surprised exclamations at the very different mental images prompted by the same story. These enthusiastic debates encouraged more children to read the stories and see what they imagined the characters to look like.

- Memories of contexts in which they had read or heard the same story.

    This category surprised us. Children were frequently reminded of times and places when they had heard the story or book read to them. Kelley's drawing of her grandma reading her *Sing a Song of Sixpence* as she rocked in the rocking chair "when I was two years old" (see Figure 7–5) shows her powerful memory of that shared storytime.

The children in Nancy Winterbourne's class obviously see reading as a way of connecting their own experiences and memories to those in the books they read!

Visual Response in a Multiage Classroom

Jill Ostrow's multiage classroom is also built on a child-centered philosophy of literacy instruction. Visual responses to literature are a vital aspect of their

FIGURE 7–6

reading workshops. In March 1994, my second year in the classroom, I interviewed several of the children about their processes and responses as they worked.

Eight-year-old Laura was midway through a condensed version of Robert Louis Stevenson's *Treasure Island* (1990).

"Can you tell me what you're working on, Laura?"

She showed me her careful pencil drawings of images from the story (see Figure 7–6) and said: "Well, Jill told us to draw a picture of a thing that we had in our mind from our book, and I drew the things down here. That's Pew, and he's blind and he got trampled by horses, and that's Flint, and he died of a stroke. And then, that's Long John Silver, and that's a young sailor. Jim climbed into the apple barrel to eat apples, and then, they came and sat down and he could hear their conversations."

Laura and I exchanged recollections of different parts of the story—scenes that were scary, suspenseful, or funny. Laura talked about picturing herself as Jim, hearing what he would hear and seeing what he would see in the dank and smelly apple barrel. I ended by asking, "How is it different thinking about the book in pictures than writing about it in words?"

Laura's answer was prompt. "Pictures are more exciting and interesting, and I see them in my head. And when we talked about it, now JB and Josh and Rachel are reading it, and some other people want to. We might do a play, maybe, sometimes."

Seven-year-old David had chosen a very different book to read: *The Littles Take a Trip* (Peterson 1968). He explained his drawing (Figure 7–7) this way: "This is my vision of the dad looking around trying to find a shelter place and this is my vision of when the dad gets stuck in mud. And Tom's trying to help him out." Like Laura, David found his "vision" encouraged other kids to want to read the book and compare their images with his.

Six-year-old Megan was chuckling over her drawing as I slid into a child-sized seat next to her. "Can you tell me about what you're working on now, Megan?"

"Jill asked us to draw a picture of what comes to our mind when we read our book. I'm reading *Fox All Week*" (Marshall 1984).

"And so tell me what came into your mind."

"I picture Dexter, and where he found a box of cigars. And then, um, smoking them. So, their face turned green and blue!"

"Oh, my gosh!" I laughed. "And what's this? What's this bird doing?"

FIGURE 7–7

Megan joined my laughter. "It's Frog and so he has to have his face turn blue, 'cause he can't turn green 'cause it's already green!"

Clearly, she was enjoying the chance to relive vivid elements of the story. She told me that she liked to draw things about the stories she read because "you use your imagination more."

"Oh, how's that?" I asked. "Why do you use your imagination more?"

"'Cause it comes to your mind. The picture in your mind." She paused a moment, then nodded her head for emphasis. "Yeah!"

Children in Jill's class have the option of using visual response pages similar to the ones that are a part of Nancy Winterbourne's class. Because of the range of ages in Jill's class, Jill and I created two kinds of response sheets: one with both sections on one page, as Nancy and I had done in the past, and one with a full page for each section. We found that even the older children usually chose the sheets that gave them more room to explore their mental images through drawing.

When I read aloud the story *The Kuia and the Spider* by Maori author Patricia Grace (1981), we found their memory images helped them make strong personal connections to a very different culture. The Kuia, or grandmother, in the story is constantly bickering with the spider that lives in the corner of her kitchen, as they compete about everything from the quality of their weavings to the pleasure they take in their grandchildren's company. In her visual response, Laura was particularly struck by the images of the Kuia and the spider weaving (see Figure 7–8). Their bickering also called to mind similar bickering she had taken part in: "It reminds me when me and my sister fight."

Just as the Kuia makes "mats" (baskets) for each of her grandchildren, with their names woven into the design, Anna's grandmother knits them all sweaters with their name in it. Her drawing shows her grandmother sitting on a chair, with a huge ball of yarn and knitting needles in her hands. "It reminds me of my grandma," Anna wrote. Her response caused several children to add their stories to the conversation, as they, too, related to their grandmothers' making special items for them.

As we reviewed transcripts of whole-class discussions and interviews with children as they worked, Jill and I were impressed with how important the talk around their visual responses was to their understanding and appreciation of the stories. In some ways, the drawing and writing of their mental images were conversation starters: all the children came to these discussions with something they were eager to share. As we listened to these conversations and looked closely at their responses, we found ourselves assessing the children's literary experiences in a broader way.

Taking a New Direction

Based on what I've learned in these two classrooms, I have redefined what is possible with regard to children's comprehension and the connections they make to the stories they read. I have been led in new directions for helping them become confident, passionate, lifelong readers. I now ask myself a series of seven questions when I'm assessing students' reading. These questions are only a beginning; I invite you to revise and add to them as you learn from the experts in your own classes.

1. What evidence do I have that the student is able to relate the reading to other human experience, especially her own? (This shows whether she can generalize and abstract information as well as enjoy the book in a more personal way.)

Your Name _Laura_

Title of the Book _The Kuia and the Spider_

Today's Date _11-7-93_

....

Draw a picture of your favorite part of the book.

Write one or two sentences explaining your drawing.

The Kuia Weaving

The Spider weaving

FIGURE 7–8

2. What evidence do I have that the student is able to accept responsibility for making meaning out of the literature and the discussions? (This helps me understand whether he is an independent meaning maker, genuinely making the kinds of connections that help him form opinions about his reading, or depends on others to tell him "what it means.")

3. What evidence do I have that the student is able to recognize differences and similarities in the visions offered by different texts? (Does she draw on her reading history and adjust her thinking as she acquires a wider range of ideas and views?)

4. What evidence do I have that the student is willing to express responses to what she reads? (Is he timid? cautious? restrained? What can I do to help him?)

5. What evidence do I have that the student is able to tolerate and accept others' opinions of the work? (Is she receptive to the ideas of others, willing to change her mind and treat a beginning response as a draft, to revise her opinions? Is he able to challenge others in a cooperative rather than combative way?)

6. What evidence do I have that the student is able to *enjoy* the reading? (Can she say why she likes it or doesn't like it?)

7. What evidence do I have that the student can take another perspective in his reading? (Even very young children can learn to see things through another's eyes. Is this happening? What can I do to encourage it?)

This new view of reading puts children's imagination at the center of their literacy experiences. In the past, school instruction has tended to view imagination as an *escape* from real life and the business of learning necessary skills. Fortunately, today's educators are looking for alternative notions of what schools can be. More and more classrooms like Jill's and Nancy's are helping students use their literate voices in new and imaginative ways.

References

Allard, H., and J. Marshall. 1977. *Miss Nelson Is Missing.* Boston: Houghton Mifflin.

Berger, B. 1984. *Grandfather Twilight.* New York: Philomel.

Dahl, R. 1977. *Charlie and the Chocolate Factory.* New York: Bantam/Skylark.

Esrock, E. 1986. "The Inner Spaces of Reading: Interviews with John

Hawkes, Carlos Fuentes, and William Gass on Visual Imaging." *Journal of Mental Imagery* 10(2):61–68.

Grace, P. 1981. *The Kuia and the Spider.* New York: Penguin.

Hodges, M. 1984. *Saint George and the Dragon.* Boston: Little, Brown.

Hubbard, R. 1996. *A Workshop of the Possible: Nurturing Children's Creative Development.* York, ME: Stenhouse.

———. 1993. "Time Will Tell." *Language Arts Journal* (November).

Karolides, N., ed. 1992. *Reader Response in the Classroom: Evoking and Interpreting Meaning in Literature.* New York: Longman.

Marshall, E. 1984. *Fox All Week.* New York: Puffin/Pied Piper.

Ostrow, J. 1995. *A Room With a Different View.* York, ME: Stenhouse.

Pape, D. L. 1988. *The Book of Foolish Machines.* New York: Scholastic.

Peterson, J. 1968. *The Littles Take a Trip.* New York: Scholastic.

Purves, A., T. Rogers, and A. Soter. 1995. *How Porcupines Make Love III: Readers, Texts, Cultures in the Response-Based Literature Classroom.* New York: Longman.

Rosenblatt, L. 1982. "The Literary Transaction: Evocation and Response." *Theory Into Practice* 21(4):268–77.

Say, A. 1988. *A River Dream.* Boston: Houghton Mifflin.

Stevenson, R. L. 1990. *Treasure Island.* Step-Up Classics. New York: Random House.

8

Reading the Image and Viewing the Words: Languages Intertwined

Irene C. Fountas and Janet L. Olson

Introduction

In Susan Sanchez's fourth-grade classroom, talk is allowed and encouraged as an important medium of learning. The students acquire much of their knowledge by questioning, arguing, discussing, and sharing. And this talk needn't feed through the teacher; the children have learned to speak and listen to each other. They seek peer feedback, pursue varying viewpoints, and value the dialogue that fuels their learning about themselves, others, and their physical and social world.

Students explore relevant and interesting topics using a variety of processes and disciplines. For example, as they investigated the Westward Movement, they hypothesized, predicted, estimated, classified, drew, painted, read, listened, talked, and danced. And they shared their learning by creating a Westward Ho museum, which included hands-on displays, beautiful artwork and music, charts and maps, poetry and stories. To add to the power of their presentation, they each stepped into the role of a character of the times, creating a costume and engaging in authentic dialogue with student and parent visitors.

Just as her students collaborate in their learning, their teacher collaborates in her teaching. Susan Sanchez's constant interest in discussing teaching and learning brought her together with Janet Olson, art specialist, and Irene Fountas, language arts specialist. Together the three of us explored the relationship between reading, writing, viewing, and drawing. We asked, How does visual expression inform verbal expression, and how does verbal expression inform visual expression?

Close Viewing Informs Writing

We wanted to investigate to what extent the visual image could be used as a tool to inform student writing, so we began by introducing the students to Vincent Van Gogh's painting *Bedroom at Arles* (Petrie, p. 71). We told them that Van Gogh was a very famous artist who lived about one hundred years ago in France. In order to place the painting in context, we also showed them a few of Van Gogh's other paintings, including self-portraits (Petrie, pp. 68 and 88) and *The Yellow House* (Petrie, p. 70), a painting of the house in which his bedroom was located. We asked the students to look very carefully at *Bedroom at Arles* and then to write a description of it. These writing samples were saved for comparison with their later writing.

The next day we began "close viewing" the painting with the students. Using Edmund Feldman's (1981) four-step method of visual criticism, we led the students in a group discussion. By describing, analyzing, interpreting, and evaluating Vincent Van Gogh's painting of his bedroom at Arles, the students experienced the critical process, reading the image through a gradual process of translation.

We began by asking, What do you see in this picture? The students took turns naming everything they could see, beginning with the largest and most obvious things—the bed, the chairs, and the table—and gradually moving to the smaller, less obvious details. It became a challenging game to see an overlooked detail that no one else had noticed. We invited further analysis by encouraging them to suggest descriptive words that would enhance our under-standing of the image. Words like *dusty, scratched, bleached, chipped,* and *worn* were applied to the texture of the floor, for example.

Gradually the students moved to a deeper level of inquiry and began to test their interpretive skills. They asked why, what, how, and where questions: Why are there two pillows on the bed? Where might the doors lead? How could the floor have gotten so scratched? Students were encouraged to explore a wide range of possibilities, as long as their suggestions were reasonable and plausi-ble in terms of the visual clues in the painting. For example, one student suggested that the door on the right side of the picture was possibly a storage closet or at least not used regularly, because the foot of the bed was partly in front of the door—an interesting hypothesis, based on a very subtle visual clue.

Feldman's final step of visual criticism is the evaluation of the image. Based on the entire discussion, the students addressed the value or the meaning of the painting. They shared a range of possibilities. (Noelle: "I think Mr. Van Gogh's room was interesting because of his neatness." Cory: "I feel he is happy and sad. He could be happy with himself and his pictures.")

After this close viewing, we asked the students to do a detailed drawing of Van Gogh's painting, keeping a list of the "special" (i.e., not obvious) words they thought of while they were doing so.[1] The copying in this particular case

---

[1] *Art teachers are sensitive to the issue of copying and image, but copying is a valuable tool for learning. The British artist David Hockney explains: "Copying is a first-rate way to learn to look because it is looking through somebody else's eyes, at the way that*

was akin to reading aloud. When students read a paragraph aloud, they are essentially "copying" the words of the author, trying out the words the way the author expressed them. Similarly, our students were reading *Bedroom at Arles* aloud visually, in order to help them translate the visual language into a verbal one.

Irene C. Fountas &
Janet L. Olson

Finally, we asked the students to write a second description of Van Gogh's *Bedroom at Arles*. We encouraged them to refer both to the print of the painting and to their own drawing and to consult their list of special words.

Comparing the before and after writing examples, we saw that close viewing of the image dramatically improved the quality of their writing. Whether a student's drawing skill was superior, average, or even less than average, he or she effectively communicated an understanding of the image in the second writing, demonstrating a deeper level of comprehension and meaning. We offer below a number of specific examples.

Ezra

Ezra's description before close viewing:

> *It has a bed against the wall and a chair and a table beside it. There are five pictures on the wall and one mirror. It has only one window. There is a wood floor. It has another chair and one closet. It has something on the wall too.*

Ezra's drawing is shown in Figure 8–1.
Ezra's description after close viewing:

> *Vincent is a man with a neat bedroom. It has only one small window which gives a tiny bit of light. On one side of it is a mirror and on the other side is a nice pitcher. Above his wooden bed, with a beautiful red blanket, are four very nice paintings. Beside his bed is an old chair made of green straw. On the other side of the room is a towel with red and blue stripes hanging on a rusty old nail. Under the mirror is a fine wooden table with a drawer and on it are a pitcher, bowl, vase, cup, plate, ink and a brush. On either side of the room there are closets. Next to the table is a nice old wooden and straw chair. Behind his bed is a hook with clothes on it. The room has a wooden floor and blue window frames. From this you can see that Vincent likes old things.*

person saw something and ordered it around on paper. In copying, you are copying the way people made their marks, the way they felt, and it has been confirmed as a very good way to learn by the amount of copying that wonderful artists have done." (Wilson et al. 1987, p. 193)

Old
Warm
neat
reged
strong
Wooden
Dirtiy
lots of thing
Putty

FIGURE 8–1

Our comments on Ezra's writing:

Ezra's first piece is short—six simple, choppy sentences. He includes only some of the items and few descriptive words. After his close viewing of the painting, Ezra writes a significantly longer piece, using more fluid language in twelve interesting and complex sentences. He notices many more items in the painting, expands their description (noting color and texture), and indicates their exact location. Ezra even talks directly to the reader in his final sentence, using his description to venture a conclusion about the painter himself.

Mara

Mara's description before close viewing:

There are pictures all over the walls. The bed is small and wooden with two white pillows and a blanket. There's a chair right next to the bed. Against one wall is another chair with a little cushion on it. Next to the first chair is a small wooden table with some cups, a pitcher and bowl, and an ink bottle on it. Behind the bed are some hooks with clothes hanging from them. There's one more hook with some wrinkled up cloth hanging from it on the opposite wall. On the wall next to it is a small mirror and a green window pane. The floor is wood stripes. There are two doors on either side of the room. The paintings on the walls are

tidy
angled
dirty
cozy
cuddly
like curves ⌣
-weird
bleeding
unclear pointing
stiff
closed in
nerd
shapes
clues
mysterios
question

FIGURE 8–2

good. The window looks 3-D. It looks neat, tidy, small and very interesting. The doors look open. It looks like it would be nice to live in. The walls are deep, deep blue. I think he painted the paintings on the wall. The window is a sort of forest green. The cushions look very comfortable. It looks like Vincent Van Gogh enjoyed living there, it looks so very, very, very, very, very cheerful. The mirror looks so clear that you could see anything with it. There is a small drawer in the table with a white round handle.

Mara's drawing is shown in Figure 8–2.
Mara's description after close viewing:

Van Gogh's bedroom is cozy, warm, comfortable and still. He definitely liked the color blue and wooden things. I think he liked it there. It's very interesting. He has two chairs, two pillows, and two closets, so I think he kept one of each for his grandmother when she came. You need a door to come in, so that means there are three doors in his room. Now let's describe what objects are in Vincent Van Gogh's bedroom. There is one bed with high sides on the post. The bed is made out of light brown smooth wood. There are two fluffy and cozy off-white medium-sized pillows. There is a dark red, stiff comforter knit by Van Gogh's grandmother. There's also an off-white sheet. Two walls are light blue and the other walls are dark blue. The walls were plastered with paint brushed over them. The paint is furiously chipping off the wall. Don't leave, there is still more. There's one rectangular clear mirror hanging on the dark blue wall. Oops, that reminds me, there are five paintings hanging on the wall with wooden frames. I think Van Gogh painted them himself. There's one pull-in window with green panes. Once again it has a thick wooden frame. Right above the bed is a wooden rack. It has blue clothes and a hat hanging from it. There are two, sorry not wood but straw, chairs with velvet cushions on them. They look pretty comfortable. There is one wood, yes, wood table with a drawer that has a white handle on it. There is a blue vase, blue pitcher, and blue bowl on the table. On the table are one brush, two ink bottles, some food on a plate. In a cup in the drawer are some paints and paintbrushes. And, you guessed it, a wood floor.

Our comments on Mara's writing:

Mara first makes a fairly extensive list of items in a narrative chain of similar sentences. She provides exact locations and uses many descriptive words. Following close viewing, her writing shows a dramatic change in style; a new voice emerges as she talks directly to the reader and introduces the personality of the painter into her description. More precise, more interesting descriptive words are evident; she chooses words like *furiously, stiff, smooth, off-white, rectangular, clear, straw,* and *velvet.* The second piece is significantly more vivid and more engaging.

Daniel

Daniel's description before close viewing:

The floor of the room is a dirty brown wood. The bed is made out of wood. The legs of the bed are three to five inches tall. In the corner there is a desk with four legs and one drawer. On top of the desk there are brushes, bottles of gin, a plate of custard, a pitcher, a bowl, a jug of water, and a glass of water. There are two pillows on the end of the bed with white sheets and a red blanket. Above the desk there is a push-out window with eight sections of glass and framed with wood. Beside the window there is a mirror hung up with wire and a nail. There are five pictures up on the walls. There are two chairs each with green cushions. There are two closets in the room.

Daniel's drawing is shown in Figure 8–3.
Daniel's description after close viewing:

The wood of the bed is light brown oak wood. The bed has four legs, about five inches tall. The mattress on the bed is very thick and fluffy. The sheets are a white fabric. The big fluffy blanket on the bed is a red velvet blanket. The two pillows on the end of the bed are big and fluffy with many wrinkles. The bed is very big and comfortable. This is the bed of Vincent Van Gogh. The desk in the left-hand corner of the room has a square top. On the desktop there is a pitcher and bowl, the pitcher is mostly filled with clean, clear water to wash your hands and face with. The color of the pitcher and bowl is a light blue. Next to the pitcher and bowl is a jug full of clean, good drinking water. Before the jug there is a white empty glass. In front of the glass there is a little saucer of a creamy custard. On the other side of the pitcher and bowl there is a brush with brown and yellow bristles. Behind the brush there are two bottles of gin with black corks. The desk has four legs made out of redwood. The desk also has one drawer probably with paint and paintbrushes in it. The drawer has a little tiny knob, to help you open the drawer. This is the desk of Vincent Van Gogh. Next to the bed there is a chair made out of light yellow wood. On it there is a green fluffy cushion. This is the chair of Vincent Van Gogh. Next to the chair in the lower left-hand corner there is a tall blue closet door. There is also another closet door before the bed. On the left of the first closet, hanging up on a nail, there is a towel made out of terry cloth, with blue and red stripes. Above the desk there is a pull-in window with eight sections of glass framed by wood. In back of the bed there is a coat rack with three blue coats and one big straw hat hung up. Above the rack there is a picture of a place framed by wood.

FIGURE 8–3

Above the bed there are four pictures: two portraits of some people and two all blue framed with big fat lines. Next to the window there is a mirror framed with wood. I think Vincent should be happy with this room because it's so clean. The floor of the room is wood and clean. THIS IS THE ROOM OF VINCENT VAN GOGH.

Our comments on Daniel's writing:

Before the close viewing, Daniel wrote a one-paragraph, rather dull list, including many items in the painting but with little exactness and few descriptive words. Following the close viewing, the writing triples in length, becomes very organized, and takes on Daniel's personal voice as a writer, with complete description and vivid vocabulary. He also introduces a stylistic element, a repetitive refrain after each section of his description. The varied, complex sentences differ markedly from his first piece. His vocabulary is much more precise, and he attends more to texture, using words like *thick, fluffy, wrinkles, clean, clear,* and *creamy.*

Close Reading Informs Drawing

We also wanted to investigate to what extent a selected piece of literature could be used as a tool to inform student drawing. If a drawing is a means of thinking and processing information, of communicating what is known and understood, and of relating oneself to a body of knowledge, then a more complete and/or more expressive and better-composed drawing provides another window for understanding the complexity of student thinking and communication skills.

When the students in Susan Sanchez's class read a piece of literature, they talk about its language and ideas. Their learning is broadened by coming to understand how others interpret language, events, or situations. After reading a section of a book, the students often revisit the text with their teacher, focusing on particular ideas, concepts, images, or language patterns. This conscious contemplation or mindful reading (Peterson and Eeds 1991) enables students to construct a deeper understanding. Shared inquiry like this encourages students to analyze, interpret, and puzzle over how the author chooses and arranges words to convey meaning. By examining and weighing possible interpretations through talk, students discover new layers of meaning.

Susan Sanchez's class that year was studying a Newbery Honor Book, Natalie Babbitt's *Kneeknock Rise* (1987). We selected this book as the medium by which to explore the relationship between the students' close reading and close drawing. Would a close reading of a portion of text improve the students' ability to reconstruct, translate, or view its meaning as an image?

In the story a boy named Egan goes to visit his fussy, nervous Aunt Gertrude and calm, methodic Uncle Anson in a village at the foot of a strange cliff called

Kneeknock Rise. Anson's only brother, sickly old Uncle Ott "who does nothing but read books and write verses" has disappeared again, so Egan will use his bedroom while he visits. Cousin Ada, a most disagreeable child, has made Egan's greeting a very unhappy one, so he is eager to get to his bedroom for the evening. We asked the students to read Babbitt's short description of Uncle Ott's bedroom—"Egan felt better when he saw the room. There was a cot against one wall, with pillows and a pile of worn and comfortable quilts. The corners of the room were cluttered with little heaps of books and papers, and on a large table, beside the usual pitcher and bowl, there were quills and ink and an old pipe. The cloth on the table was stained with blots and pen scratches. It was all very untidy and interesting" (p. 17)—and then, using fine-point, black drawing pens, to draw a picture of Uncle Ott's room with as much detail as possible. These drawings were saved for comparison with their later drawings.

The next day, we did a "close reading" of the same paragraph. The students gave careful attention to the details and images as they elaborated on the meaning of words and phrases such as *worn and comfortable, cluttered,* and *untidy.* They discussed various interpretations, examining the author's careful choice of words.

Then we asked the students to draw the room a second time. The differences were dramatic, as the examples below show.

George

Our comments on George's drawing before close reading (see Figure 8–4):

George provides a bird's-eye view. There is a heap of papers in one corner

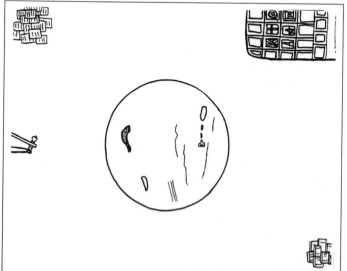

and a heap of books in the corner diagonally opposite. The table (on which only a pipe and bottle of ink are identifiable) is the main focus of the composition; however, the detailed, intricately designed quilt in the upper right corner shifts visual weight to the right side.

Our comments on George's drawing after close reading (see Figure 8–5):

George once again provides a bird's-eye view but adds a bit of three-dimensional perspective. And this time, rather than showing very separate parts, he has pulled together and unified the items into a complementary whole. In addition to the basic floor

FIGURE 8–4

plan, he shows a partial view of the walls, including a person (possibly Egan) appearing at an open door, a window, and a picture. Many more details are provided—the pitcher and the bowl on the table, a second pillow, and a rolled-up quilt or blanket at the foot of the bed—and the room is obviously much more "untidy." George has also added some personal interpretations to the drawing, which are not mentioned in the paragraph but make logical sense. There is a chair at the side of the table, and clothes are scattered on the floor.

The composition is beautifully balanced: the visual weight of the objects on either side of an imaginary line drawn down the center of the image is equal. The placement of the clothes on the floor also shows an innate sensitivity to visual balance, five objects at the lower right, one small object slightly to the upper right, and one pair of pants on the left. The table, the main focus of the drawing, is moved slightly to the left, in order to compensate for the weight of the bed and the rolled-up blanket at its end. This drawing reflects Uncle Ott's presence.

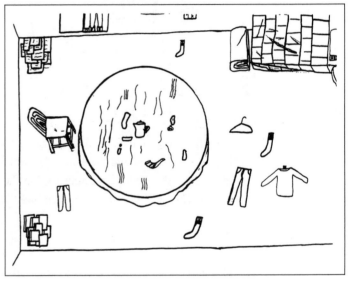

FIGURE 8–5

Lizzie

Our comments on Lizzie's drawing before close reading (see Figure 8–6):

Using a portion of her drawing paper and thin, delicate lines, Lizzie offers a bird's-eye view of the room with the essential objects lined up around the periphery. The bed is in the upper right corner, a folded quilt at the foot, and papers are stacked in the upper left corner. She has drawn a table at the left, a door at the lower left, and a desk at the lower right. There is much open space and the room appears quite tidy.

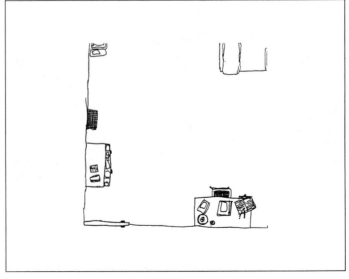

FIGURE 8–6

FIGURE 8–7

Our comments on Lizzie's drawing after close reading (see Figure 8–7):

Lizzie has taken a straight-on frontal point of view in her second drawing. She conveys a sense of three-dimensional space and her lines vary from thin to thick. This adds visual interest and indicates a new confidence with the drawing pen.

The objects on the table are clearly drawn and a clock is added. The bed is obviously a folding cot, with folded quilts and a stuffed animal. A wastebasket, two piles of paper (right and left) and a shirt that reads "Vote no! #2" are on the floor. She has included an organized bookcase (collections labeled A and B, and one book labeled Uncle Ott's), a circular rug on the floor, and a window with the shade raised. The desk is rather cluttered and the chair sits on top of a pile of books.

Noelle

Our comments on Noelle's drawing before close reading (see Figure 8–8):

Noelle has included all the essential elements—the bed with a patterned quilt, a table with papers piled up, piled papers on the floor—as well as some additional items—a bureau and a stereotypic window (with crossbar and curtains). The bed overlapping the bureau indicates an understanding of space.

FIGURE 8–8

Our comments on Noelle's drawing after close reading (see Figure 8–9):

Noelle's sketch is much more complete and visually interesting. The bureau is no longer included, but a closet with two doors is added to the right, behind the table, also indicating an understanding of three-dimensional space. The objects on the table are larger and more defined, and the papers on the floor to the right are less ordered than in her previous drawing. She has included an additional window, similar but not identical. More piles of papers are added at the foot of the bed, and more pillows and more patterns added to the bed design. The stool at the table probably reflects Noelle's personal experience. A shirt hanging from the window sill suggests untidiness, as does the shirt on the floor, still on a hanger.

FIGURE 8–9

Vertical lines in the background add a great deal of visual interest because of their variation. If the spacing between the lines were exactly the same, the image would be redundant and boring. The line and space variations powerfully communicate a full and untidy room.

Conclusions

Following our collaborative work in the classroom, we talked about the data we had gathered and reflected on the experience. It was clear from the students' work that the quality of their writing and drawing improved after they had engaged in close viewing or close reading. They were able to translate ideas more fully whether from a visual to a verbal product or from a verbal to a visual product. One language informed the other.

To summarize the relationship between verbal and visual languages, we constructed a model to capture the dynamic nature of the process (see Figure 8–10). The model demonstrates how the learner is encouraged to move back and forth between visual and verbal expression, letting one language inform the other. The black arrow at the top of the figure shows the various modes of expression (viewing, reading, drawing, writing) as they inform the learner. The eye in the figure symbolizes a composite of the learner's visual and verbal personal experiences on a shaded continuum from black to white. The next section of the figure shows the learner constructing meaning, with visual experiences contributing to verbal expression and verbal experiences contributing to

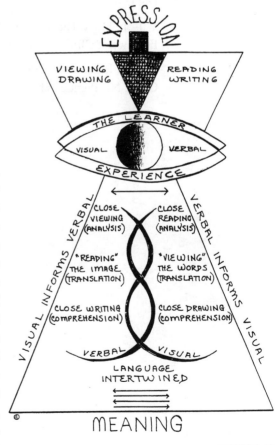

FIGURE 8–10

visual expression. When learners engage in close viewing or close reading (analysis), reading the image or viewing the words (translation), and close writing or close drawing (comprehension), the verbal and visual languages intertwine naturally, each informing the other, resulting in fuller and more complete meaning.

Irene C. Fountas &
Janet L. Olson

References

Babbitt, N. 1987. *Kneeknock Rise.* New York: Farrar, Straus, Giroux.

Feldman, E. B. 1981. *Varieties of Visual Experience.* Englewood Cliffs, NJ: Prentice Hall.

Olson, J. L. 1992. *Envisioning Writing: Toward an Integration of Drawing and Writing.* Portsmouth, NH: Heinemann.

Peterson, R., and M., Eds. 1991. *Grand Conversations.* New York: Scholastic.

Petrie, B. 1974. *Van Gogh: Paintings, Drawings and Prints.* New York: E. P. Dutton.

Wilson, B., A. Hurwitz, and M. Wilson. 1987. *Teaching Drawing from Art.* Englewood Cliffs, NJ: Prentice Hall.

Wilson, B., and M. Wilson. 1982. *Teaching Children to Draw.* Englewood Cliffs, NJ: Prentice Hall.

9

Parallel Journeys:
Exploring Through Art and Writing
in Fourth Grade

Peter von Euler

Keeping an observation journal has changed the way I teach and the way I look at my world. I use my journal to examine my practice, reflect on successes and failures, and look more closely at my environment. My fourth graders also keep observation journals, unlined sketchbooks in which they sketch, reflect, record, and imagine. Together we have learned from each other, and like all explorers we have encountered new voices and unexpected sights.

The Journey Begins

On a raw Thursday morning my fourth graders bounced through the building on their way to artists workshop. I felt nervous. The art teacher, Karen Ernst, and I were going to give the kids sketchbooks like the ones we use as our own journals. No big deal, perhaps, but this was special, my students' invitation into the adult world, their sign that they were "journalists."

We sat on the rug in the art room. Karen introduced the journals by sharing hers:

> *I use it to guide my whole life. I write to plan my days, to work out problems I have in school, to collect my observations. We're giving these to you with the idea that they will make you better students because we feel that if you learn to look more closely, to examine your world, you will become a better writer, a better reader, and a better picture maker. These are not for doodling or cartoons or jokes. These are for your sketches, your ideas, and your imagination.*

We talked a bit about firsts. We told them how nervous we were about this introduction, because it was a first step in an exploration. We mentioned how important we felt the first page of a journal was. Karen said she often put a significant quotation or a drawing that she would enjoy revisiting on that first page. We asked the kids to give some serious thought to how they would use their first page. Then they were off.

Katie, a technically talented artist, found new freedom in her journal. She wrote of her discovery on the first page:

> *Today I learned how to use my journal. I started to sketch Zoë very detailed then I thought to myself, this is just a sketch. I don't need to make it detailed. So I decided to look at the shapes more than the texture. I think I would like to take the bottom part of her and cut it off because it doesn't feel like a picture to me.*

Katie had started on a path that would lead her into experiments and big departures in style. She freed herself from having to create "works of art" and could now explore the "shapes" and "feel" of a picture.

Lauren followed the suggestion of using a quote from a poet. She transcribed one of her own poems onto the first page:

MY LAND

> *If I could invent my very own land*
> *And be ruler of it*
> *If I could invite*
> *Only people I like*
> *And tell them what to do*
> *There would be houses*
> *That you can build yourself*
> *And cars for kids*
> *That you can paint on*
> *There would be shops and malls*
> *Where everything is free*
> *And parachutes*
> *So you can fly*
> *Fly anywhere, even back to the normal world.*

Explaining her selection, she drew a parallel she would mention throughout her journal:

> *I chose this poem that I wrote to be on the first page of my journal because it is sort of about a dream land. I used my imagination to write it. That is what this journal is. Ideas. Imagination. Thoughts. Anything really.*

From the moment I read Lauren's first page, I knew that I could expect remarkable connections between art, imagination, ideas, and writing. My class and I were beginning a journey on which I was as much a passenger as a navigator.

A Bit of Background

At the beginning of the school year, four classroom teachers at our school had formed a first-through-fourth-grade team that would work with the art teacher, Karen Ernst, on a pilot project we called Infusing the Arts into the Writers Workshop. Our goal was to expand our writers workshops to encompass and encourage more types of expression, not to improve art skills. We felt we could improve literacy by broadening kids' views about how they can express feelings and ideas. I joined the project because I wanted to draw on the seeming magic of our school's artists workshop, where students wrote in their artists notebooks with greater power, honesty, and true emotion than they wrote in my classroom. I sensed that the blending of literature, pictures, and words allowed a more natural flow of language, a flow that blended streams from both the head and the heart.

At the end of a two-day planning session in August, I wrote in my own journal:

> *These two days make me very excited about the possibilities for this year. I see every time I observe or take part in an artists workshop that different voices come out of us. People sound so different from the way they talk when they write about and read their words in the context of art. A greater depth is revealed. They read from beneath their surface voice.*

I had been keeping a journal for about a year. Its "unlinedness" led me to use it in a way I hadn't anticipated. I took to sketching as well as writing—both to help me focus objectively on a particular subject and to banish the clutter of ideas from my head. I observed, recorded, and wondered about our project:

> *Questions remain—will this just be an extended artists workshop? Will the excitement of paint just overpower writing? Will we just need to get up some momentum in writers workshop for it to carry over? So far I'm not sure how much concentrated writing went on. I'd like to hear more entries first. I did hear this: "I like what I wrote today—it really made sense for a change."*

Many of my later decisions resulted from my early questions. For example, I set out from the start to be more vigilant in using the words of my students as my guide. I was determined to keep careful track of their comments, both oral and written. I think their awareness of my note taking, how much I hung on their words, affected their attitude throughout the year. They saw that what they said could change our course.

Routines: The Silent Write

Neither Karen nor I had envisioned that the observation journal would become the focal point of our pilot project, but in fourth grade at least, it did. By the time that day in February arrived, my kids were already experienced journal writers. They had begun to see the value in the habit of writing.

At the start of the year, concerned about the competition between picture making and writing in my writers workshop, I had changed my routine. I set aside at least ten minutes at the start of our daily artists/writers workshop for silent journal writing.

Immediately I noticed two significant effects: first, many kids opted to continue writing in their journals once we moved on to independent projects. Journal writing became natural and necessary. Second, by having ten uninterrupted minutes for myself, to write, reflect, and plan in *my* journal, I became a better model. Kids saw me writing, which I had rarely managed to do in the busy moments of a bustling workshop. Frequently I was writing for the class, knowing that I would share what I'd written. When I did, they heard my writing voice as well as what was on my mind. I became more committed to my own journal and more focused on the ideas expressed in my students' journals. They in turn became more excited about the possibilities and proud of their increased productivity.

Journal Leads: Getting Our Writing Going

As we began work in the observation journals in February, I continued the ten-minute sessions at the beginning of every workshop. Each day I tried to give kids leading questions or suggestions for themes. I usually gave them several possibilities, the last of which was always "your choice." This kept things flexible: it was less confining or contrived than a story starter, but also less open ended than just saying, Let's write. I tried to relieve the stress that some children (and adults) feel when staring at an empty page, forced to generate ideas. I really wanted them to develop a habit and an ease in writing. I also wanted them to get beyond simply retelling a day or event. I asked them to respond to quotes from stories we had read, make plans for the day or week, rewrite a lead or a journal entry, comment on a current event, write about what they noticed in the hallway galleries.

Sometimes topics I would otherwise have presented in a more teacher-directed way I now posed as questions for their journals. I also began to see things I usually introduced through whole-class brainstorming as perfect leads for journal writing. For example, I wanted to get kids off the idea that poems had to rhyme, get them to expand their definition. I suspected that they knew more than they revealed in their poetry, that they were somehow limiting themselves through habit. The writing they did when presented with the journal leads *What do you think a poem is? What do you look for in a poem?* led to more focused and crafted responses.

Here's Lauren's:

I think a poem is something that grabs you, and it gets your attention! I think a poem is something you can become, or travel to. All of a sudden you'll be able to travel into the words, or the poem. You will be able to feel a happiness inside of you. And you will just let the poem take you away.

Liz wrote,

When I look at a poem, I look for emotion, great deep feeling. I look for describing words that explain the whole poem. I look for happiness, sadness, and anger deep down in the poem. I look for the meaning of the poem and see if I feel and understand the way the author does.

Many of their responses were so thoughtful, I merely recorded their ideas in my journal. They seemed committed, eager to explain, and involved in the subject.

Imagination's Place: Writing What You Can't Say

After touring the all-school art exhibition one day, a fourth grader expressed surprise at how imaginative the younger kids' art seemed. Karen sent this comment back as a question: "Do you think that younger children have more imagination than fourth graders?" The fourth graders said yes! They offered all sorts of reasons why they had lost their imagination. I took notes on their responses, not knowing what else to do or say. I felt a bit sick inside at the notion of nine-year-olds grounded for life in the world of fact and law. Did this response reflect what they *thought* we wanted them to say, that somehow imagination was for those less able, that it was pretend, the approximation resorted to by those who couldn't do the real thing? Most years I would not have been able to endure that feeling. This year, because I felt more like a researcher and an explorer, I saw it as an opportunity.

When we returned to my classroom. I told them that the conversation interested me, because I wondered how an artist could function without imagination. I asked them to think on paper about what imagination really is. Andrew, one of the kids who had so confidently shared why they no longer needed to use their imagination, wrote:

Imagination is what helps you do things,
lets you fit oceans into
small jars, elephants into
pencils, turn covers into
secret bases, turn lumps of
clay into awesome statues.
You can do $3^3/_4$ of everything with your imagination, it is
like a backpack crammed
with homework for school!!

In writing this poem in his journal, Andrew drew on all sorts of experiences, synthesizing his life in his definition. He incorporated lines from poems he'd heard ("elephants into pencils"); he recalled his recent clay creations, the games he played at home, and the work he had been doing in math with fractions; and he created his own metaphor, the overloaded backpack. To me this revealed an imagination flourishing, overflowing, not fading. It also revealed a powerful new voice for Andrew, confident, expressive, and unrestrained. Finally, this confirmed for me the value of observation journals as a place for my students to write what they couldn't always say. Whereas moments before they had agreed that their imagination was waning, now in their journals, where they could think, connect, and wonder in semiprivate reflections, their imagination resurfaced.

As much as possible I tried to link the experiences in the artists workshop with the writing they did in their journals. Leaving their imagination behind, whether in the art room, or in the younger grades, was a loss I hoped we could forestall.

Writing That Helps You Know the Picture

We had an understanding in our class that anything worth doing was also worth writing about. This meant that any pictures they made during our daily artists/writers workshop had to be accompanied by some form of writing. The artist might reflect on the process of creation, journey into the picture, respond to what she sees in the picture, or compose a poem inspired by the picture. I accepted many types of writing and encouraged or applauded new ways of responding. Over time I began to notice that the responses were becoming a bit static or predictable: When I look at my painting I see. . . . So as a journal lead I encouraged the artists to experience their picture without their sense of sight. Carson took his picture of the Toronto Blue Jay's dugout (Figure 9–1) and wrote:

> *If I went inside my picture and had to use my other senses (without sight) I would smell tobacco. I would hear loud chewing noises. I would hear the crack of the bat. The crowd with a sudden burst of cheering. The radio announcer yelling. I would spit out the last piece of tobacco from my mouth and then go celebrate with the team.*

FIGURE 9–1

Carson does more than just list sensations in this short paragraph, he lives and captures a moment. Every time I see his picture now, I see *him* in that dugout, yelling, spitting, celebrating.

Journal Journeys: Transported by Writing and Looking

Throughout the year my journal became more and more valuable to me, sometimes my compass, sometimes a friend. It often carried me through difficult or grumpy moments and in doing so sometimes generated a lead. For example, this entry:

> *We're in art.*
> *Nothing is seeming artistic to me today. Scratch that, nothing is—scratch that, I don't feel artistic today. Scratch that, I don't feel schoolish today. I don't feel social or interesting today. Usually this time of year feels clear and orderly to me. Now it feels forced and rushed. What is the logical culmination of this last hour and a half? What should we write about?*

prompted this lead:

> *If you could be somewhere else, sketching right now, where would you be? What would you see?*

I tried whenever possible to let kids see that I sometimes used my journal to work through a problem. I wanted them to see that the focused thinking involved in the act of writing also helped push aside distractions and could lead them to a clearer path. The image of travel or journeying arose from these personal discoveries.

In order that our new, unlined journals not become only a sketching place, I began giving homework assignments. At first I asked my students to sketch for a certain amount of time, fifteen minutes to half an hour, and then to write about what they noticed. The class took to it with gusto, and so did I. Soon, however, I began to see new needs:

> *I think I need to have some ideas to propel this project, so that it doesn't get boring or so that the quality of discovery doesn't deteriorate out of lack of demands or structure. One thing I'd like to encourage is taking new perspectives—looking at things from unusual angles or positions—like the underside of a table, the couch from the ceiling, a tree from the base looking up. I'd also like to encourage the idea of doing a study. Taking a particular thing, person, sight, and really taking a close hard look at it. Maybe doing a sketch of it, a memory-sketch, a painting, a description, a poem. Maybe the way to do it is to pick a theme for the week (each individual picks his own theme), work around that theme, and then share the study and observations on Friday.*

The following week we began what we called Journal Journeys, week-long projects in which we sketched things related to a theme and then wrote about our sketched observations. My hope was that we would arrive at a new place by the end of the week, that our looking and reflecting would make us notice more around us, give us the feeling that we were rediscovering our world. Kids approached this assignment in many ways. Some sketched their room, the furniture in their house, plants they thought looked interesting, or views from different windows. Sam, for instance, started sketching his violin from different angles, ending the week with a sketch of his closed violin case (see Figure 9–2). That Friday, I asked the class to take us on a written tour of their week-long journey. Many wrote as though they were leading a group through an art gallery. Sam had a slightly different approach:

> *This week I'm off to the violin world where colors are music and words aren't reality.*
>
> *"All aboard," said the conductor. "This train's leaving." I thought to myself, any time now, and I'll be stringing.*
>
> *When I arrived on my private train club car, I saw a whole new world of 4 huge strings on one instrument. I couldn't even see the whole thing. The chin rest was very real, the best part of the violin.*
>
> *The next day I saw a bow leaning on that same violin. This time the instrument is up, down, and across so many lines . . .*

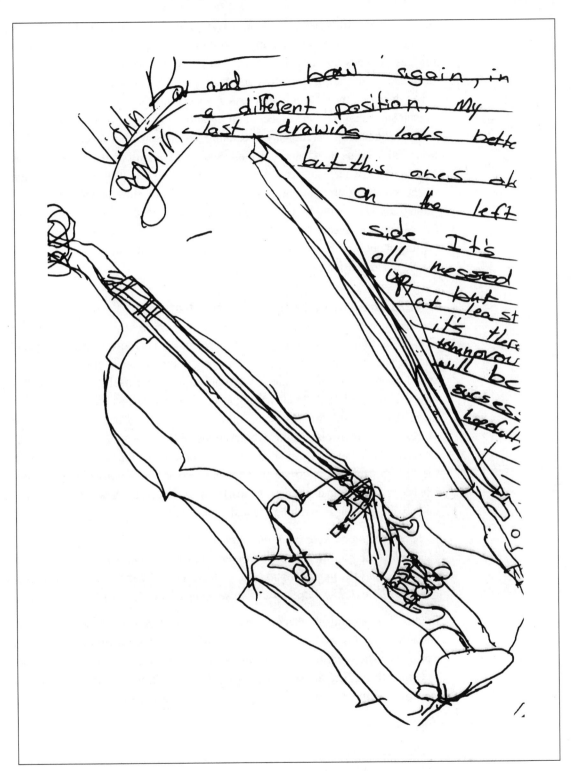

Violin body and bow again, in a different position, My last drawing looks better but this ones ok on the left side It's all messed up but at least it's there tomorrow will be success. hopefully

FIGURE 9–2

Sam's earlier efforts had always been very grounded. Writing seemed a chore. His observation journal gave him a new outlet and purpose. He put great effort into his sketches but they also seemed to propel his writing, which needed to keep pace with the greater detail and feeling.

As they took these weekly journeys, my students began to look more closely at their surroundings. One aspect of observation certainly involves concentrated looking. Sketching the things you examine requires another layer of attention: you need to focus on what you actually see, looking with an objective eye. You need to draw what you see, not what you expect to see. The major advantage of the sketching assignments was that they made us slow down. Rather than letting the world whiz by us, we forced some of the world to flow through us. We captured at least a few of the images around us, and the follow-up step of writing about our observations challenged us to really pay attention, both while we sketched and afterward.

Seeing the Moon Tangled in the Branches

One of the things I had observed with envy in the art room in previous years was the phenomenon of new voices emerging as kids wrote about their art. This year I happily discovered that it was not the art room itself that created this effect: it resulted from kids' writing what they saw. Apparently I had never given them this opportunity or encouraged it enough. I began to hear those voices in my own classroom. Observations didn't always come out as full-fledged poems, but what struck me as I read through the journals was how open the kids became, both to striking images and to image-provoking phrases. Lindsay's journal had poems on nearly every page. Even when she wasn't composing, she was searching for and capturing images:

> *I drew the moon tangled in the branches of a tree that's in our yard. I was looking out the window and then I saw the moon, with a satellite over it, and the moon was tangled in branches, so I stored the picture in my brain and then I drew it in the morning.*

Lindsay had become a collector of pictures and picture-evoking words. To me, her accompanying sketch is far less significant than the process of seeing and storing that she describes and the obvious pleasure she derives from the phrase.

On another page, she sketched a wrapped present, with a ribbon, bow, and tag, followed by a poem that may not have filled her with pride:

PRESENTS

Pretty and nice,
It's something great,
That everyone wants,

Something neat, cool, and kind,
Presents are presents.

After writing the poem, she thought a bit on paper:

> *I just let my mind flow in this poem. I like writing poems because I can*
> *use my imagination. Also because my mind is free and I can write down*
> *anything I want on a piece of paper. I think poems are very creative and*
> *wonderful.*

As though this reflection had gotten her in the mood, inspired her to be more creative, she then penned another poem at the bottom of the page:

> *Presents are the to and from,*
> *The life of presents seems to go far,*
> *The life of love goes farther,*
> *Stops, go's, stops, go's,*
> *Love is more important than presents,*
> *Love is feelings,*
> *Hopes and joys*
> *Love always takes your heart away,*
> *And makes you happy all day!*

Reaching the bottom of that page, I felt as though I had been inside Lindsay's head. I could only guess at the true process, but I had seen her go from the surface of the present, the wrapping paper perhaps, into a deeper place. A little tug-of-war had taken place on that paper, between the kid who just liked presents (and who doesn't?) and the kid-poet who longed for deeper gifts. One side wrote for fun and defended that approach ("my mind is free and I can write down anything I want"). The other side wrote to explore, valued creativity, and looked for something with "feelings, hopes and joys." The page itself had depth. It gave me a truer picture of Lindsay than I would have perceived if I'd only known her from what she said in class.

Drawing Out the Purple Horse: Planning a Picture While You Write

Another day my own journal entry raised a question that I passed on to my class: might their own writing serve as the springboard or inspiration for their pictures? This ran counter to my own expectation, which was that picture making propelled thinking and writing, but I thought perhaps sometimes a cart actually could pull a horse.

In a minilesson I told them a story from *Picturing Learning* (Ernst 1994) of a student whose artists notebook had contained some lines of descriptive language that sounded like poetry. When questioned, he revealed that the words were not in *response* to a picture, but were *plans* for a painting.

I suggested that my students might try to visualize a picture and then plan it in their journal. Teddy, usually a reserved or fact-based writer, wrote:

> *In my mind I see a brown horse in a stall with other horses like black ones and white and gray and one is purple. The brown horse is wagging its tail looking around. It has bristled hair and the owner is walking around. The doors are open and you can see the grass leaning one way from the slight breeze. You can feel the wind blow lightly on your back giving you that refreshing feeling. The water sparkling and the sun shining and the owner taking the purple horse for a ride.*

Teddy not only found a new voice and style in this rapidly written entry (he had previously written only reports on states, and this interrupted his survey of the mid-Atlantic region), he also found a new power and purpose in writing. As I talked with him, he "confessed" that the purple horse had not been in his original mental image; it had only appeared as he wrote. In fact, his only image when he began to write was that of the brown horse. In this case the writing actually fueled the image making in his head. This notion that writing, the actual act, can unleash images and ideas, had a powerful effect on Teddy. Suddenly he saw writing as a process of creation, not merely as a record or a retelling.

Looking Closely Requires Thought

As the process of sketching and reflecting became habitual, I found that the writers became more probing and that their thinking became more analytical. One way for them to respond to their sketches was to look critically, describe what they noticed, and think about what they liked or disliked. In other words, they could assess themselves. Even in stray moments like the one Elizabeth describes here, this analysis creeps in:

> *I was sitting in the car waiting for Joanna to get out of music. I turned to the car next to me and sketched a person that was sleeping. I like the way it turned out. I found you can see something without every detail. I almost think it looks a little better without eyes etc.*

Elizabeth has taken that normally empty time, waiting around in a parking lot, and given it value—she has discovered a drawing technique and realized for herself the meaning of "less is more."

This process of self-assessment is undeniable in Katie's self-portrait and commentary:

This week I realized that my journal journey was harder than just
drawing myself in the mirror. When I started drawing it I didn't think it
looked like me because I put in so much detail. When I look at myself I
don't see all of that, and so I look like a totally different person. I think
why I don't see it is because my face has color and that attracts my eyes
to look at color more than my detail.

Instead of congratulating herself on a beautiful drawing, Katie breaks it down. She makes the amazing observation that she has more detail in her sketch than she notices when she looks in the mirror. Then she theorizes about why her eyes don't usually see this detail, that they are distracted by color. Reflecting on her reflection in the mirror has not led Katie to be self-absorbed; rather, she is seeing herself through new, more objective eyes, and she is learning about the interaction between senses and thought.

In some cases the object of scrutiny is not the student herself and her own picture, but someone else and someone else's art. One day in the art room Chelsea decided to sketch John's painting of a barn, while at the same time observing him at work:

John made this house with much detail. John made lines with a real thin
paint brush. Then he colored over it with brown paint. But his problem
was that no one could see the lines so he asked Miss Ernst what he
should do. She told him to use white paint to show up the lines so he did.
Then he asked Mr. von Euler if he should of used black instead of white.
So Mr. von Euler showed him a window with black gates outside and said
some things turn black from their shadow. Then he continued drawing the
barn which I thought was a house. I learned a lot more about John and
his paintings by watching [him] and sketching his painting. I think he
really likes it because [of] the expression on his face and how detailed he
drew this picture. I also know he likes using the white as lines because he
said that using the white as lines was a really good idea. I think I learned
a lot about myself by drawing this picture.

An entry like this impresses me with its detail and sustained attention and also makes me wonder. What prompted Chelsea to do this study? What did she actually learn from this observation? I do know that she managed to compress time, to slow down the pace of the workshop and focus on a small part of her world. She clearly sees the richness in the act of creating a piece of art.

Paying Attention to Process

One day I asked my class if they could write down some suggestions for the second graders in our "buddy" class about how they used pictures to create is Maggie because she is caring and adventuresum and funny. I think she's abou 8 or 9.

Understanding Disability
U D

Today Slone (sălōn) came. She is in a whe chair. I must be hard for her because not a places have handicap utilitys, and because she is in a wheel chair

March 28

Writing

The way I write a poem or anything abouta pict is study the picture and then I put down on paper ho I feel about it or what I see in it for example

but some times I gest Ezetorsp lonly. I leaf left feel o, knowth ppem spcile it's lik I'ugl read read it about 10 times

the poem The I dont tree stands with one leat left and a pile below

FIGURE 9-3

poems. In the past I found that activities like this frustrated nine-year-olds. They could do something but found it difficult or annoying to have to think about *how* they did it. I just do it, they would say. In this case, however, many felt they could analyze their process. Zoë broke her method down into steps, and for purposes of explanation (if not art), she actually followed those steps in her entry (see Figure 9–3). The illustrative poem was by her own admission not one of her best, but having the art of writing down to such a science was at once impressive and a bit disconcerting. I was almost grateful for the element of mystery in her last sentence.

> *The way I write a poem, or anything about a picture, is study the picture and then I put down on paper how I feel about it or what I see in it. But sometimes I just feel or know the poem straight, and it's like I've already read it about ten times.*

Sarah, too, had begun to see the artfulness of her own process. As she finished a painting in the art room, she decided to record it in her journal. She

FIGURE 9–4

began by doing a sketch of the painting, but then decided that the tools of creation were as important as the picture. She sketched her supplies and then composed the words (see Figure 9–4).

Clip Clip Clip, her scissors go up and down munching at the paper to make the sun. Stroke, stroke, stroke the paint brush slides across the paper to make the snowy mountains with all the different colors of watercolors. Plop, she measures how tall the mountains should be. Eek, the markers plop on the paper as snow. Scratch, the pencil goes up and down, making the trees. Then she says, "I'm finished."

And the Details Are Your Thoughts

My students' apparent awareness of a bigger picture encouraged me to ask them to write about more abstract questions in their journals. The answers frequently came back in concrete terms, but it amazed me how readily my students accepted such questions. They responded to What is art? with a grandness that I would never have expected. Lindsay had this to say:

Art is your own creations. It is like explosions of bright colors on your mind. It lets you do things never done. It is like millions of little hands helping you when you create something wonderful. Without art, people wouldn't care or want to exist. They would just mope around doing nothing. Art is what created paper and pencils, paint and paintbrushes, colors and clay. It is what created everything. Art is all these things in my mind.

Lauren tackled the question philosophically, but she clearly shares the vision that art inspires thinking and that this realization develops from writing:

I think art is pictures, imagination, and thoughts. You can draw a picture with imagination in it and the details are your thoughts. If you copy art, it is nothing. It doesn't have your *own thoughts and imagination in it. It is like becoming another person instead of yourself. Copying is only good if you want to learn from that person.*

I think that art is for expressing your feelings, getting them down on paper. Showing people how you think without talking.

Where Have Journals Led Me?

Observation journals have changed the way I teach. In previous years I recognized the value of art as a form of expression, but I viewed writing as a more challenging and perhaps more important discipline. Art and writing existed as islands, two separate rooms in my school, two separate compartments in my mind. Over the course of the year, as I thought, sketched, recorded, reflected, and wondered in my journal, I went from thinking that I had been carried across a gulf to realizing that the gulf was imaginary. I came to see, through the guidance of my students, that the gap between art and writing was only a space in my mind. Elizabeth made this link in her observation journal:

> *Writing and pictures are the same. Writing is putting pictures and thoughts into words, and pictures is putting words into what you can see.*

She sees the natural connection between writing and art, one that in previous years I had severed. As an adult, perhaps I needed a vehicle to carry me from one island to the other. To Elizabeth it's a matter of common sense. It says so right in her journal.

Reference

Ernst, Karen. 1994. *Picturing Learning: Artists and Writers in the Classroom*. Portsmouth, NH: Heinemann.

10

I Look at My Pictures and *Then* Try It: Art as a Tool for Learning

Jean Anne Clyde

I have always enjoyed viewing and creating art; however, I never understood its potential as a vehicle *for learning* until I met six-year-old Douglas. I was his coteacher for his first school year and spent a second year observing Douglas and his friends in a multiage setting.

Changes Over Time

In August of 1990, Douglas appeared younger and less mature than his peers. Full of life and energy, he was a lovable child, yet one not easily understood in conversation nor easy to help focus.

Midway through his first year, Douglas became a sports columnist for our class newspaper. His first submission, "Basketball," was expressed in art (see Figure 10–1), a decision that was easy to understand given the struggles he experienced as a writer. When his piece was completed, Douglas talked about it with his friend Andy. Listening to them, I discovered things about Douglas's illustration that were not apparent from simply looking at it. Most important, the game was still being played. His picture represented a single frozen frame of an event that he continued to create as he talked. Douglas spoke knowingly about his characters' actions, even those who existed off the page. Players' motives and intentions became clear as he told about their tripping and falling and running into one another. He drew as he talked, and invited Andy to be a player. Collaborating with Andy on a finish for the piece, Douglas authored, for the very first time, a story his audience was able to read:

BascBall	Basketball
the Black	The black [team]
woe Fawl	won. Yellow
yellow	fouled.
Ah the GuHL	And the girls
WhaSaetafogh	was satisfied.

This experience was incredibly powerful for Douglas; driven by a newfound awareness of art as a tool for expressing and organizing his ideas, his once unfocused behavior changed dramatically. Soon I rarely saw Douglas without his journal. It had become a vehicle through which he was able to explore topics that were meaningful to him.

FIGURE 10–1
Douglas's first sports article, entitled "Basketball"

For several months, Douglas devoted time each day to producing page after page of characters that he referred to as his "skateboard guys" (see Figure 10–2). His drawings seemed to enable him to live the sport vicariously. Through his drawings, which some consider "primitive," he seemed to be exploring (1) the limits of the sport—the laws of physics governing skateboarding, and (2) the potential of his tool—his pencil, which enabled him to participate. Douglas's figures revealed his uncanny ability to capture movement that reflected the constant challenges he faced in trying to stay on his own skateboard.

Douglas was diligent in his search for resources to further his study. Skateboarding magazines, books on skateboarding (with text far more sophisticated than he could manage independently) that contained photos of skateboarders engaged in perilous acts, and *Skate TV,* a television program that featured real skateboarders, all provided useful information in his quest to become a better skateboarder. Nearly every day, in what appeared to be an attempt to rehearse skateboarding, Douglas composed one or more of what he called "movies," using multiple images (Hubbard 1989) of

FIGURE 10–2
Douglas's "skateboard guys"

his guys. He seemed intrigued by what was possible in this sport and driven to improve his own abilities.

Each day Douglas would flip through his fairly disorganized journal, inspecting earlier drawings. Often he would add to those drawings, quickly sketching in one or more figures; at other times, he would study his entries, squinching up his eyes as if determining their accuracy. Sometimes he would revise them. He was constantly evaluating his work, revealing his developing understanding not only of the sport but of his ability to capture it through art.

In many ways, Douglas was much like Scott, a first grader whom Glenda Bissex (1983) identified as a "self teacher." Scott worked on images of sharks over time "not to repeat but to learn and improve" (p. 96). Like Scott, Douglas's

> most important teacher must have been his own eyes—his ability to measure the work he had produced against what he had intended, to clarify that intention to himself, and gradually to find the means of realizing it. (p. 96)

Searching for Meaning in Others' Texts

As Douglas became more reflective about his own work, he seemed to develop a similar and previously unseen interest in searching for meaning in other children's work and a better understanding of the role of audience.

Early in March, Kyle shared a picture he had drawn. "I have a weather picture. It is of a tornado and the solar system. It is cool," he told his friends, describing its various components.

But Douglas objected. "Why did you say, 'It's cool?'"

"It *is* cool," Kyle defended.

"But it could *kill* somebody," Douglas noted adamantly.

On another day, Cameron shared a complex illustration he had been working on. "People are fighting over the land—a piece of land, and they are fighting in boats because they don't want to burn up the land," Cameron explained. "And I'm not done with it yet, 'cause I was gonna draw the man right here, and they had surrounded that big boat."

"How did they round him?" Douglas asked with great sincerity.

Douglas was clearly interested in *making sense of* his friends' texts. This was a significant departure from earlier days, when he had struggled so to even sit still during sharing.

Learning from Others: The Impact of Demonstration

In mid-April, Douglas's skateboarders adopted a sudden, very different appearance (see Figure 10–3). The changes were inspired by a cousin who, having grown tired of Douglas's constant requests to draw *for* him, had shown him how to draw for himself. The stylized characteristics of these draw-ings suggested that Douglas had carefully attended to her demon-strations (Smith 1988). Yet he man-aged to skillfully blend the new boxy figures, which featured profile faces, with his existing understand-ing of how to represent movement. Like his earlier figures, these skate-board guys were also enduring the struggles of remaining atop their boards.

FIGURE 10–3
Douglas's skate-boarders after "les-sons" from his cousin

Douglas's investigations into un-derstanding movement through two-dimensional art underwent many other shifts in the months that fol-lowed; as his interests changed, so did the subject of his inquiries and the compositions he used to explore them. Each new sports figure re-vealed Douglas's developing awareness of the associated physical qualities. When he returned to school in the fall as one of twelve second-year students in a multiage classroom, his inter-ests centered around a variety of figures and activities, from super-heroes to wrestling. Douglas's su-perheroes were usually wielding weapons and were constantly on the move. His World Wrestling Federa-tion (WWF) figures featured overly developed, muscle-bound torsos, with visible pectorals and swollen biceps and quadriceps (see Figure

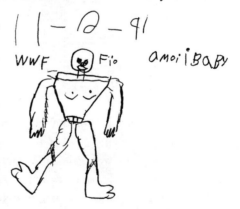

FIGURE 10–4
One of Douglas's muscle-bound World Wrestling Federa-tion guys

10–4). Prominent muscles were also a feature of the weight lifters he drew. Douglas was aware of the distinct differences between the physiques of every-day Joes like skateboarders and wrestlers and weight lifters.

Using Drama, Art, and Mathematics to Explore Basketball

One morning in mid-November, Douglas and his friend Richard were working in their journals at the same table, Richard on superheroes stories, Douglas on basketball. Douglas quickly drew and cut out a basketball player—number 19 (see Figure 10–5), then began work on a second—number 48. He added wrist bands to this player, who had his right arm down at his side and his left raised alongside his head. Douglas quickly drew in loopy legs on this figure, then added a circle (a ball), larger than the player's head, atop the left hand, and colored in the shape. On another sheet of paper, Douglas drew a tall rectangular shape; on top of it he added a second curvy-sided box. This was his basketball goal. Douglas drew a circle in the middle of the "square," a bird's-eye view of a basketball hoop. Touching the lowest point of the circle, he added some circular marks—the net (see Figure 10–6). He laid his goal on the desk, beside player number 48, which was approximately the same size, and studied them, his eyes moving from one to the other. Dissatisfied, he turned over his goal and began again.

FIGURE 10–5
Player number 19

While we might label Douglas's rejection of his goal as common sense, mathematicians would say it reflected his developing understanding of "proportional reasoning" (National Council of Teachers of Mathematics 1989), a recognition that the proportions of his two drawings—the player and the goal—were somehow "not right." To remedy the problem, he quickly drew a second goal, taller and more slender than the first, that extended nearly the entire length of his paper. It was much more proportionally accurate, given the size of his players. And rather than combining perspectives by showing the circular quality of the hoop with a net attached, Douglas's second goal maintained a single perspective, with the net hanging straight down as though the viewer were facing it.

Next, Douglas drew a third player—number 91—and cut him out. He then returned to his second player, the one with the ball in his hand, and began cutting around this drawing as well. Douglas cut between the legs first, manipulating them back and forth, as if to test their ability to move. When he finished cutting, he briefly laid number 48 beside his drawing of the goal, then stood both drawings up and moved his player through space, as though attempting to make a basket. He laid the player down, picked up his scissors, and cut out his goal.

His attention then turned to stabilizing the goal. "I gotta cut out the hoop. I gotta sit it up somewhere, like right here," he said, propping his goal up against a crate of supplies that was on the table. Douglas picked up number 91 and trimmed around him some more. Still holding number 91, he picked up the goal with the same hand, his right, and with his left hand picked up a book that lay on the table. He spread the pages of the book a bit so that it would stand without his assistance, then leaned his goal against it. When he removed his hand, the goal slid off the book onto the table. Douglas trimmed some more around number 19, then picked up number 91, glanced at it, but put it down again. He searched among the scraps and found number 48—the guy with the ball, an apparent necessity for the game he was creating.

With a player in each hand, Douglas moved them through space, making them jump concurrently several times as though playing the game. The book served as

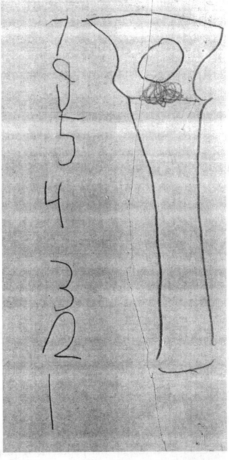

FIGURE 10–6
The first basketball goal, featuring combined perspectives

the backdrop as Douglas took his players through the motions of dropping a ball into an invisible goal that appeared to be the same height as the book. Douglas moved both players to his right hand and, with his left, leaned his goal against the book. He then slid it in between some of the pages, securing it, but making sure that the hoop part extended above the pages. He moved the players through space, rehearsing a shot; but the hoop extending above the book was apparently too high for his players. Again displaying his awareness of proportional size, Douglas folded the paper forward, perpendicular to the cover of the book. "I need a hole right there," he announced, pointing to the flattened paper with his scissors. He stabbed at the paper several times before successfully puncturing it. He tried to use his finger to enlarge the hole, but the paper tore as he did. Douglas inspected the tear, then removed the torn part, effectively shortening his goal by an inch and a half.

Eisner (1982) claims that "the process yields ideas that are not a part of the initiating conception" (p. 51). This was evident in Douglas's work. He studied the longer of the two pieces; then he overlapped the ends of the strip and, after three full minutes of struggling with the stapler, converted the two-dimensional strip into a loop, a three-dimensional hoop.

"Look, here's a hoop that you shoot it into!" Douglas grinned, as he held up his stapled loop of paper. "And you tape it on to something. And then it's a hoop, and it's either high or low." Douglas found the remains of the paper from which he had cut the goal, tore a long strip off one side of it, and attached his hoop to it with a staple.

"Does this really look like a hoop, Richard?" Douglas asked, holding his hoop up for his friend to see. "Richard, does this really look like a hoop? You know, like a basketball hoop?"

Richard glanced in Douglas's direction. "Make a ball, man."

"He gots a ball," Douglas said, holding up number 48, the player with the ball, for Richard to see.

"You want to be able to drop it through there, man," Richard reminded him.

"Oh, I know what you're talking about! Draw a ball and cut it out!"

Having determined, with Richard's help, that he needed a ball that was separate from the players, Douglas rushed to the supply drawer. "I'm gonna *make* a ball!" He returned with a strip of paper, roughly four inches by nine inches, and overlapped the ends of the strip. The edge formed when he did so was circular and looked much like his original two-dimensional ball; yet this "ball" was actually a short tube. He had not yet noticed that the round yet elongated shape was larger than his hoop. But Richard had.

"That'll be too big, Douglas."

"No, it won't," Douglas mumbled, not particularly convincingly. However, he began wadding up his paper, as if responding to Richard's prediction. "I *can't make* a ball!" he concluded, clearly exasperated. "But I *do* have to make one and cut it out."

Douglas left the table again and returned with a six-by-nine-inch sheet of yellow paper. He drew a small circle in the middle of it, announcing, "Now, there's a basketball," as he cut out the small round shape. With his hand over the top of his player's hand, he clasped the flat "ball" and, propping his 3-D goal up with his other hand, dramatized the player's leap toward the goal. He released the two-dimensional ball over the basket. "He made a hoop!"

Six-year-old Geoffrey had been watching all of this and offered to make Douglas "a *real* ball." Douglas accepted and watched as Geoffrey fashioned a ball by wadding up a piece of paper much smaller than the one Douglas had used. When he finished, he flipped the ball through Douglas's hoop. Douglas tried out the basketball next, successfully dropping it through the hoop several times. Then he began playing the game with his figures. I asked him to talk about what he was doing.

"Well, it's like a five-feet hoop. That's the hoop I got at home," Douglas said, stopping to write numerals on his goal, beginning with 1 at the bottom (see Figure 10–7). Douglas's decision to begin marking the height of his goal from the bottom up was significant, indicating an awareness of how one measures height. "That's five feet," he said, tapping his pencil on the numeral five. "You can have it big if you want, or small if you want. It can only go ten feet high . . . I'm gonna put a six feet . . . seven," he said, adding six and seven to his goal. "That's seven feet. And here's me right here [*indicating number 91*]. And I can only go this high," he continued, holding number 91 so that his feet were about at the two-foot mark on his goal.

"Oh, you can only go that high?" I asked.

"Yeah. If my feet can go five feet, I can slam dunk it," Douglas replied, holding number 91 so that the figure's feet matched the five-foot mark on his goal.

Here Douglas revealed his familiarity with two other mathematical concepts. His comment that the closer he got to the basket when he played the more likely he was to score suggests a basic understanding of the notion of probability. In addition, he was aware of the relationship between his own height and how high *his* feet had to be above the ground before he would be able to score with the goal at seven feet.

I had not realized that one of Douglas's players represented himself. "It's my suit I wear when I play basketball," he informed me. His friend Andre was number 19. Douglas was connecting his life with the substance of his inquiry and in the process demonstrating his knowledge of yet another mathematical concept: that numerals can be used nonmathematically as identifying symbols.

For many months, I had seen Douglas create and cut out figures that he manipulated in space and that seemed to serve as props for whatever sport he was "playing." I had been convinced that this activity served some important function in Douglas's inquiry into how to become a better skateboarder, but I wondered about its usefulness in learning about basketball. "Tell me more about your decision to cut them out," I invited. "How'd you decide to cut 'em out?"

"Because when I draw them, I want to play with them, and I can't play with them when they're in paper," Douglas informed me.

I asked if it mattered how he drew them, if they could move anyway.

"It doesn't matter how you draw 'em. They can still move."

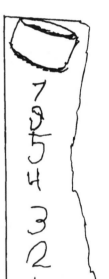

FIGURE 10–7
Sketch of Douglas's 3-dimensional basketball goal

"Is there anything you've learned about basketball from doing this?" I asked.

"Yeah. I learned how to slam."

"Tell me how you do that. How do you learn from doing pictures?"

"'Cause I look at it for a long time and then I try to do it . . . and then I can do it sometimes."

"Do you look at your pictures and then try it or do you look at . . ."

"I look at my pictures and *then* try it."

As he had with his skateboard guys, Douglas was using his basketball guys, his artwork—drawing players, cutting them out, and moving them through space—as a tool for his own learning. This *transmediation*—from movement (physically playing the game) to using art to create miniature replicas—enabled Douglas to reflect on his own performance and to more fully understand the demands of the game. According to Harste (1994),

> *Thinking of things, in speech, in art, in music, in math, is a first step in making them happen. . . . Real growth occurs when learners see their efforts in one area . . . as answers for how they can solve a current problem. (pp. 10, 12)*

Moving from Artist to Critic

I had noticed that Douglas often "revisited" his pictures. I wondered if he could talk about that decision, and asked if he ever changed his pictures. "Sort of," Douglas replied pensively, as he looked at player 19. "Sometimes."

In her study of preschool literacy, Rowe (1994) discovered that

> *as children shifted* social *stances from constructing texts as authors to responding to audience questions and comments about their work, they were also encouraged to shift* cognitive *stances from using literacy to reflection on it. (p. 93)*

And so it was for Douglas. When asked *about* his drawings, he changed stances, from artist to critic of his own work (Eisner 1982).

Here's the next segment of our conversation:

JA: When do you change 'em?

D: When I think they don't look right and I don't think they can be anything, I erase the whole picture.

JA: How do you know if they don't look right?

D: 'Cause I might have drew his leg wrong [*looking at player 91 still in his hand*]. Like I drew this leg big and this leg small?

JA: And why'd you do that?

D: I didn't *do* it because I wanted it to *be* like that.

JA: So is that right, do you think? [*I am immediately uncomfortable with my question.*] Do you like it like that?

D: Sort of. [*His tone is unconvincing. He begins folding under the figure's left foot, which extends past its mate.*]

JA: So now you're making him different?

D: I gotta fold him up and staple him.

While Douglas's quickly drawn characters had worked well as props for his sports event, stepping back to discuss them caused him to evaluate his work; he saw that there were inaccuracies.

But I had an alternative explanation for Douglas's having made the legs different lengths; one seemed to be foreshortened. "That's interesting, 'cause you know what it looks like to me? It looks like he's turned so that this leg's sort of *away* from him. So this leg's away from me, and this leg's closer so that looks— let me show you what I mean." I went across the room, where I stood facing him with feet shoulder width apart. "See how my legs look the same length?"

Douglas nodded. I pivoted so that my right leg was behind my left a foot or so, asking him to watch what happened, hoping he would see the difference in perspective.

When Douglas still seemed confused, I repeated my demonstration, this time even farther from him. I concluded my second lecture with, "Artists do that so they can show that people are turning. When they put this leg shorter, it looks like the leg is back a little ways. That's what yours looked like to me."

It was time to change groups. "Douglas, we have to change groups now. What are you gonna do with your guys?"

"I'm gonna play with them over in Artspace," he informed me as he stapled up the foot of the subject of my soliloquy.

The Benefit of Shifting Perspectives: Developing of New Insights

Harste, Woodward, and Burke (1984) argue that

> *involvement of alternative available expressions of language . . . and communication systems (language, art, math, music, drama, etc.) allow language users to psychologically and sociologically shift stances and get a new perspective on their knowing. (p. 216)*

In the course of this single event, Douglas continually shifted perspectives, and the impact of those shifts on his work was obvious. He used art to create players and props, yet his shift to "thinking like a mathematician" played an important role in his reflection on the accuracy of his drawings. Dramatizing the game helped him better to determine the appropriate height of his goal. And while discussing his playing, he once again became a self-critic, determining that the representation of his player's legs was problematic and needed to be changed.

Drawing with Douglas: Insights into His Understanding

In an effort to understand Douglas's decision making during what appeared to be effortless composing in art, I later asked him to show me how to draw one of his basketball guys. I drew alongside him, doing my best to keep up, often asking questions. Douglas was patient, even though my pace slowed him down considerably.

Douglas had already begun work on his player when I joined him, having drawn some lines to indicate a torso. He added legs and a line indicating the length of his guy's shorts; I asked how he knew how long they should be. "'Cause I watch basketball and I see how long the legs should be," Douglas replied. He then added a series of geometric shapes to his guy's shoes. "It's just the shapes on the shoe," he told me. "It means they're good players."

He made dark lines near the player's shoulders to indicate "those shirts that they wear . . . that don't got sleeves," then used little sketchy lines when he drew the arms. "Tell me why you used those lines there."

"'Cause I try to be a artist. Artists use lines." Douglas paused to study his figure. He added a basketball hoop to his picture, then used a solid line to make a circular shape for his player's face. "I messed up on the face," he said, erasing the original line. He redrew it using short, light strokes—artist's lines. I asked how he knew he had messed up. "'Cause I drew it all the way over here like that?" Douglas explained, tilting his head and using his hands to indicate that his figure's head was too far to the right.

I asked about the position of his player's arms. "See, he's slam dunking, like this?" Douglas said, standing to demonstrate the action.

I noted the dark oval shapes on the inside of each of Douglas's guy's arms, where they connected to the body. "That's the muscles," he said. Next Douglas labeled his guy's jersey—Bulls—indicating that the player belonged to his favorite team. As we colored our respective uniforms, I noted some little lines I had not seen earlier. They were above the knees, visible through the shorts he had drawn.

Douglas explained. "Ya see, he's turning around like this?" [*He demonstrates the stop-action pose.*] It's makin' him look look like, well, like that . . . to make him turn around. Like, I got a leg right here?"

"Like his shorts have a wrinkle in them, you mean?"

"Yeah."

Douglas had so carefully studied the sport that he understood the impact of movement on a player's clothing, the way the fabric from his uniform fell around his legs.

Next he drew a net and lines indicating the floor "he jumped off of." I asked if he was playing outside. "No, he's playing for real," Douglas replied. "He's playin' a real game." As usual, Douglas had created a context for his player.

Next, responding to a classmate's observation that, "You need hair," Douglas added a "box" to the top of his player's head. "Looks like he's having a good time," I commented.

"He's not having a good time," he told me with great seriousness. "He almost fell. You know, when they fall down? He almost fell."

"He did?" I was rather surprised to hear this, given the smile he had drawn on his player's face. But I did not think to question him about this anomaly. "How did you know that?"

"'Cause I saw a movie, and he was slam dunking? And he catch the ball from this guy in front of him, and he almost tripped. And then he jumped up and slam dunk," Douglas said, providing yet another indication that he had constructed a context around this player.

I asked Douglas which player he had drawn. He paused, then decided he had drawn Michael Jordan and began to write his name in a shortened form—Mike. He struggled to write it, at first putting a *g* in the name, then erasing it and adding a *k* instead.

Next Douglas drew a vertical line extending from the base of his backboard to the court below, "the stick that holds the basketball hoop." Finally, Douglas finished coloring his guy's uniform. This use of color was quite new for Douglas, and I asked about it.

"I wanted to be a artist so bad, and I wanted people to draw me

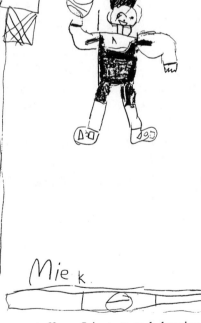

FIGURE 10–8
The player Douglas created when I asked him to show me how to draw one of his basketball guys. (Some of the details were lost when he decided to color his player's uniform red.)

stuff? And they got tired of drawing me stuff, so I just started drawing for myself," Douglas told me. "My cousin showed *me* how to draw. She puts colors in her drawings."

"She does? Is that what made you think to use colors?"

"Yeah."

"So what do the colors mean?"

"Well, they make 'em look, ya know, better, and they make 'em look—I use colors to make 'em have clothes on."

I asked Douglas to talk about what he referred to as "ardiss's lines," how he learned to make them. "I practice for a long time," he said with great seriousness. He concluded his drawing (see Figure 10–8), saying, "And that's how I do my artist's drawing."

I asked him whether he ever studied players, and he said he looked at basketball cards.

Jean Anne Clyde

126

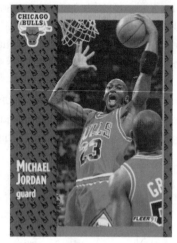

"I just keep on lookin' at two of 'em. 'Cause if I look at *all* of 'em at the same time, I'm not gonna be able to draw their bodies."

I was fascinated by Douglas's decision to set parameters around his inquiry. By choosing just two photos, he limited his investigation, made it manageable.

While I never learned which two cards Douglas used as his primary resources at that time, I recently located several at a local shop that I

FIGURES 10–9
Basketball cards featuring Michael Jordan. Given the similarities to Douglas's spontaneously produced drawings, he may have used these or others like them as resources for his inquiry.

suspect influenced his inquiry (see Figure 10–9). Although he did not use them during the events described here, the impact of his careful observation of these or similar cards seems evident. The cards appear to have served as demonstrations that influenced Douglas's understanding of the game, the players, and the drawings he used to represent them. They also helped to explain why Douglas's players rarely had hair, and why they nearly always sported smiles.

Different Purposes, Different Drawings

As language varies by the situation of context (Harste, Woodward & Burke 1984), so, it seems, does Douglas's art. Comparing the drawing Douglas produced for the purpose of "teaching" me with those he typically produced for his own purposes, we see obvious differences. Each of the figures created for the game was generated in less than a minute and captured a real sense of movement or motion. But when he slows down the process for me, we come to appreciate even more about what this young child has internalized about the sport and those who play it.

In Douglas's work we see ample evidence of revision, indicators of the new understanding he has developed through his use of art as a tool for thinking and learning. His insights span a broad range of topics, from physics to mathematics to how to be an artist . . . all occurring within the context of his stories or "movies" and inspired by personal experiences from his life.

Hubbard (1989) asserts that

as each of us attempts our search for meaning, we need a medium through which our ideas can take shape. But there is not just one medium—productive thought uses many ways to find meaning. (p. 3)

It seems that we have only just begun to understand what is possible when art is viewed as a tool for exploring and extending our understanding. Douglas is compelling proof that this "way of knowing" is worth investigating further.

References

Barnes, D. 1991. *From Communication to Curriculum.* Portsmouth, NH: Heinemann.

Bissex, G. 1983. "The Child as Teacher." In *Awakening to Literacy,* edited by Hillel Goelman, Antoinette Oberg, and Frank Smith. Portsmouth, NH: Heinemann.

Clyde, J. A. 1994. "Lesson from Douglas: Expanding Our Visions of What It Means To 'Know.'" *Language Arts* 71:22–33.

Eisner, E. 1982. *Cognition and Curriculum.* New York: Longman.

Ernst, K. 1994. *Picturing Learning: Artists and Writers in the Classroom.* Portsmouth, NH: Heinemann.

Harste, J. 1994. "Literacy as Curricular Conversations About Knowledge, Inquiry, and Morality." In *Theoretical Models and Processes of Reading,* 4th ed., edited by Martha Rapp Ruddell and Robert B. Ruddell. Newark, DE: International Reading.

Harste, J., K. Short & C. Burke. 1989. *Creating Classrooms for Authors.* Portsmouth, NH: Heinemann.

Harste, J., V. Woodward & C. Burke. 1984. *Language Stories and Literacy Lessons.* Portsmouth, NH: Heinemann.

Hubbard, R. 1989. *Authors of Pictures, Draughtsmen of Words.* Portsmouth, NH: Heinemann.

National Council of Teachers of Mathematics. 1989. *Curriculum and Evaluation Standards for School Mathematics.* Reston, VA: NCTM.

Rowe, D. W. 1994. *Preschoolers as Authors: Literacy Learning in the Social World of the Classroom.* Cresskill, NJ: Hampton Press.

Smith, F. 1988. *Understanding Reading.* 4th ed. Hillsdale, NJ: Erlbaum.

11

Reclaiming the
Power of Visual Thinking
with Adult Learners

Ruth Shagoury Hubbard

Every child is an artist. The problem is how to remain an artist once he grows up.

—Pablo Picasso

Making images is as natural to humans as speaking. Pictures are a way to communicate, think, express, and explore, just as words are. As soon as we begin to make sense of *verbal* language, we also start to sort the many images that surround us into *visual* language and thought. The chapters in this book speak to the importance of helping children build on their abilities to be "whole thinkers," using all their mental tools as they invent meaning from what they see and hear around them in the world.

But what about adults? Too many of us have had our image-making skills taught out of us, as our thinking has been channeled into verbal solutions in traditional classrooms. Most of my adult students have learned to be embarrassed by their artistic efforts rather than to delight in an expanded repertoire of thinking possibilities. My aim as a teacher educator is to return visual expression as a natural language to everyone, to help the adults I work with use this means of expression in all the ways they use verbal language.

Visualization and Reflection

When I talk with other teacher educators about what our goals are for the would-be teachers we work with, the theme we return to again and again is *reflection*. Good teaching has at its heart the ability to be aware of our thinking as we work through ideas and to use that awareness as a guide for what we do. I encourage my interns to become good teachers by using all the mental tools at their disposal. They fill yearlong journals with their reflections on what they are reading, writing, observing in classrooms, and mulling over in their mind and on the responses they receive from their mentor teachers, their fellow

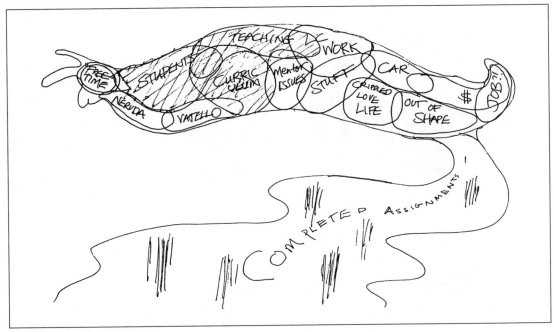

FIGURE 11–1

students, their instructors, their students. In our weekly seminars, we talk through what we are noticing, asking: What does this mean? What did I learn from this? What would I do differently next time?

The written reflections we share in these seminars help us process what it means to learn and to teach. But sometimes the words become too comfortable, let us keep too safe a distance from experience. As Leo Lionni notes, our discussions too often become "spinning words about words, without looking back to the images that precede words and the feelings that precede both" (1984, p. 732).

In order to get at these images more clearly, my colleague Andra Makler and I ask our students to visualize what is actually occurring in their brain as they teach. What are the main elements of their thinking? *Where* in their mind do they visualize their thinking? The resulting drawings force us to go deeper than words and lead to richer understanding of the complex acts of teaching and learning. We find that the most spontaneous ideas emerge when we have the students complete the drawings during class time, quick sketches in ten minutes or less. This frees them to put their preconceived standards on hold, using symbols and sketches rather than working to create beautiful finished "products."

These "drawings of the mind" have occasioned some powerful learning experiences; often the return to images uncovers new ideas hidden as metaphors. Rob drew his brain as a giant slug (see Figure 11–1). His categories bring out the concerns that lurk in the back of his mind: Will my car start? Will

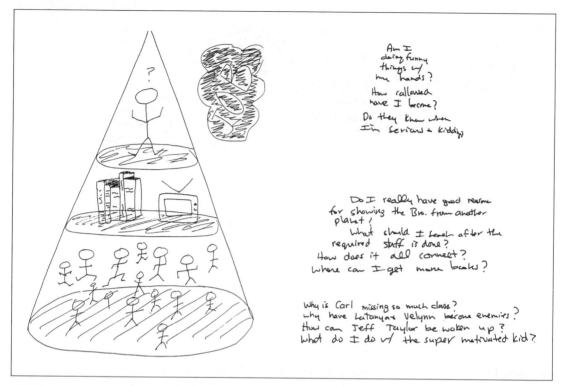

Am I
doing funny
things w/
my hands?
How calloused
have I become?
Do they know when
I'm serious + kidding?

Do I really have good reasons
for showing the Bro. from another
planet?
   What should I teach after the
required stuff is done?
How does it all connect?
Where can I get more books?

Why is Carl missing so much class?
why have Latanya + Velynn become enemies?
How can Jeff Taylor be woken up?
What do I do w/ the super motivated kid?

FIGURE 11–2

I get a job? These concerns may drag him down, but at the heart of his thinking, shaded to show the most activity, are the three overlapping areas of students/teaching/curriculum. Discussing his drawing, Rob told the seminar group that as he drew, he realized these categories weren't separate in his mind and overlapped into other areas as well. The curriculum grew out of his students' needs, for example, as well as his own teaching strategies, and was affected by issues with his mentor (cooperating teacher). He also discovered that his teaching wasn't isolated from his graduate coursework.

Hannah drew her brain in three layers, the images side by side with her accompanying inner dialogue (see Figure 11–2). The bottom layer is filled with students—not students generically, but the individuals she has come to know and care about: "Why is Carl missing so much class?" "Why have Latanya and Velynn become enemies?" Curriculum concerns fill the narrower space above the students: "Do I really have good reasons for showing *Brother From Another Planet?*" "Where can I get more books?" Finally, at the tip of Hannah's mind as she teaches are fleeting thoughts about self-presentation, which she represents with a figure of herself under a question mark. "I'm asking, What about me?" Hannah explains. "Am I doing funny things with my hands? Do they know when I'm serious? when I'm kidding?" When Hannah began her drawing, she intended to represent a pyramid, but as she drew, she turned it into a dunce cap, reflecting her uncertainties with her new teaching assignment. By naming her self-images and self-perceptions, she welcomed others in the class to talk about their insecurities and thus realize how natural it is to wonder about how your students see you.

Visualization and Literature

It isn't only preservice teachers who can broaden their understanding through visualization. In my literature classes, I talk about mental images as a tool for achieving a deeper understanding of whatever themes or concepts we are exploring. One class I teach, Narrative and Voice: Themes of Gender and Culture Across the Life Cycle, is an elective for people in masters programs in public administration and counseling psychology as well as teacher education. Besides reading novels of our own choosing, we read two novels together, relying on discussions, writing—and images, too—to create meaning from them.

One summer session, we all found it difficult to begin to talk about the painful slave narratives explored in Toni Morrison's moving novel *Beloved* (1987). As an alternative, I asked the students to take out their journals and sit quietly for about five minutes, jotting down a list of the random images that came to their mind when they thought about the story. The room became immediately quiet. Lisa's list, typical of the responses, recalled vivid pictures and emotions:

hot, dirty, gray, unpainted wooden house
quilt—two orange pieces—happiness
shadows—holding hands
people—not being clear about their own needs
tree on back, follow the blossoms
blood—on the back, birth
powerless
Baby Suggs

To help them focus on these powerful images, I then had them form groups of four to six people, gave each group a large piece of newsprint and a box of crayons, and asked them to create a visual depiction of the images they had noted. Once the initial panic subsided, they set to work. Some groups created collagelike posters with a main compelling image—shadows of the characters Paul D., Sethe, and Denver holding hands, for example, and other images filling in the edges. Other groups created a single symbolic image incorporating the essence of all the images. One surrealistic drawing showed a huge chokecherry tree, blood dripping from branches and blossoms, each limb flowering with painful images of slavery: butter churns, bridle bits, spilled milk, scarred backs.

As we worked on these visual depictions, the talk growing out of the shared work led us to create new meaning. "Let's link this together with the river—I didn't even have that on my list, but look at how often it's come up now. We

can have it change color from a blue to a brown, dirty river as it connects our images." Eavesdropping on the groups' conversations, I saw clearly the power of breaking out of typical literature discussions and venturing into unknown territory: letting images lead to meaning rather than beginning with words.

After this initial whole-class drawing venture, some students felt permitted to include what was for

FIGURE 11–3

them a more comfortable form of thinking in their journals. Mark's journal had until then been filled with verbal reflections on the reading, but now he began to use drawings to find a deeper level of connection. As he sketched Paul D. "dressed up in a collar," he thought of the clerical collar of another character in the book and of how this "man of God" was similarly enslaved—by his racism and inability to see the humanity of Paul D., Sixo, and other characters (see Figure 11–3).

Quickdrawing and Writing

Students don't have to be accomplished draughtsmen like Mark in order to use drawing in their thinking and learning processes. I introduce "quickdrawings" to my writing classes as a way to help students access their images and use them as a springboard for working with words to create meaning. I ask my students to experiment with this strategy early on. In many writing workshops, the initial hurdle is often, What can I write about? We spend much of our first session talking about possibilities, sharing stories and topics we might like to explore. After we have all had a chance to share a story with the whole group and a couple of additional tentative ideas with a partner, I ask everyone to pick a topic and write about it for twenty minutes. Next, rather than focus immediately on the writing, I ask them to take five more minutes and do a very quick drawing or sketch of one image that stood out in their mind as they wrote, stressing that they don't have time to make a finished drawing, that they may use stick figures, focus on one aspect of the image, or render it symbolically. I then ask them to share both their writing and their drawing with a partner. The visual expressions of the images in their mind often help students connect different details of their experiences or find a new focus.

Maria was writing about a childhood memory of trying to snatch pomegranates from a tree guarded by a determined neighborhood boy armed with a Japanese beetle. Her first draft began with a description focused on Rick:

> *As Rick leapt from his leafy guard post by the tree I countered his move as if a grenade had exploded in front of me. His brown sweaty arm extended toward me with the small, buzzing beetle furiously battling the air. Responding to my retreat, Rick settled back and crouched in front of the prized tree.*

In her quickdraw, Maria rendered a huge Japanese beetle tethered by a string to the smaller image of Rick in the background. After sharing her writing and drawing, her next draft had a new lead:

> *The emerald airplane dipped, soared, and dove as if aiming directly for me. Japanese beetles were Rick's favorite defense against a marauder who determined to snatch even one pomegranate from its prickly branch. The tree was on our property, but Rick, a neighbor, deemed control as ownership. He guarded his bastion in front of the pomegranate tree with only one of these emerald-colored fruit-sucking Japanese beetles, its body reined in by a single strand of thread looped around a spiny black leg. His fingers whitened as he gripped the thread even more tightly, determined to fend me off with the beetle in flight. The fearsome attacker was a harmless hard-shelled bug flying desperately in circles to escape its unseen tether.*

The details of her remembered image stand out in her revision, from the spiny black leg of the beetle to Rick's white knuckles as his fingers grip the thread. Maria returned to quickdraws often in her writing process, using them to help her relive and recall memories.

After I have introduced quickdrawing as a possible tool, it becomes an option for students to use if they wish. Some students experiment with it further in class and in their journals, while others store it away for "someday." But I always make it clear that visual solutions, processes, and experiments are a welcome part of the learning process.

Spontaneous Images

Donald Murray starts his day by writing in his daybook; other writers, theorists, and creative thinkers record their daily musings in journals, notebooks, diaries, and sketchbooks. Artist Julia Cameron (1992) calls her "morning pages" her primary tool of creative recovery. My journal is a large sketchbook filled with notes, drawings, and taped- or stapled-in word processor printouts. I encourage my students to choose a journal strategy that works for them—lined or unlined

Reading Comprehension : Journal   6/27

Interesting point when Rosenblatt stated, "Teachers of English tend to consider themselves defenders of a lost cause, keepers of an imaginative or emotional oasis in the midst of our materialistic, science-ridden life.

Indeed, I have felt just like this at times, especially when in my Jr/Sr English class we were

FIGURE 11–4

paper; bound or loose-leaf pages; written on a computer, in pen, in pencil, or using combinations of writing and drawing implements.

Journals are a means of reflection, an important tool in my classes. We use them in and out of the classroom, recording our reactions to what we are reading as well as to the discussions and projects we work on when we are together. Sharing my own journal with my students, opening them up to what is possible, encourages them to be more playful in their thinking and reflections.

Many of my students rediscover the fun of cartoons. Jim laced his reading comprehension journal with caricatures of the authors we read and the relationship between their theories and his image of what it means to be an English teacher. In one such reflection (see Figure 11–4), he drew himself as the defender of a lost cause—a Teacher of Literature—mocking himself for the ways he was inadvertently turning kids off to literature. During a ten-minute quickwrite in a language acquisition class, Leah created the Dreaded Allomorph, a dinosaur shown overtaking a small band of students, who fight back by heaving books at the technical language monster (see Figure 11–5). Word

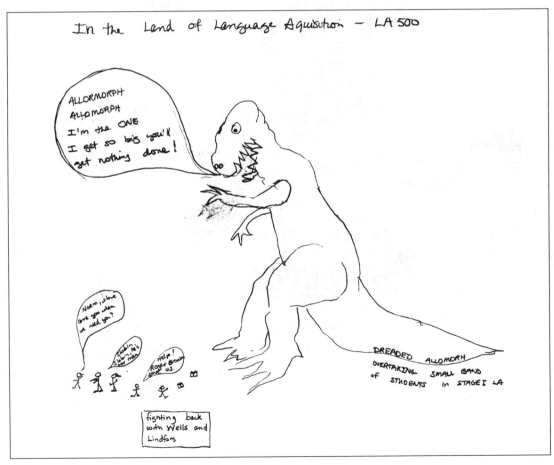

FIGURE 11–5

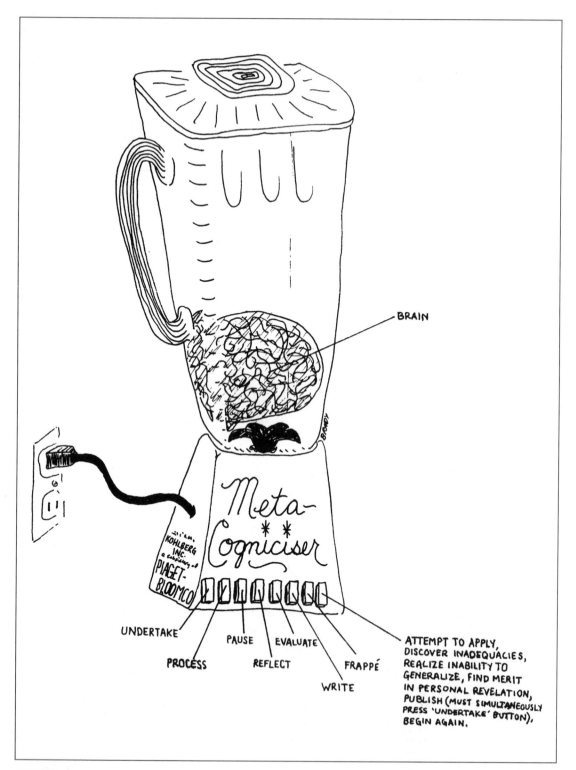

FIGURE 11–6

bubbles over the heads of these dwarfed students show them calling for help from the theorists they are reading: "Noam, where are you when we need you?" cries one, while another looks to Roger Brown to "save us." Two act as cheerleaders, chanting "Slobin, Slobin, he's our man." Besides making us laugh, Leah's cartoon helped us sort out the ways linguistic readings give us language and vocabulary to understand language development in children in new ways but can also act as a barrier to understanding. The metaphor of technical vocabulary as a huge monster who "gets so big you'll get nothing done" helped bring into open discussion a genuine difficulty in the class so that we could examine it and find ways to deal with it.

Students often experiment in ways I haven't thought of. In one Classroom Learning and Teaching seminar, we all wrote weekly response papers and brought copies for everyone to read and discuss. Kelly was the first to break out of the verbal format we were all employing, keeping to her one-page limit by creating the Metacogniciser (see Figure 11–6). The brain in this blenderlike appliance suffers the inadequacies of the hierarchical models of thinking levels we had been reading about. Kelly demonstrates her sophisticated thinking playfully, complete with in-jokes: the manufacturer of her appliance is "Kohlberg Inc., a subsidiary of Piaget-Bloomco."

Drawings like Kelly's allow reflection to get beyond stratified, linear thinking. Certainly the words are vital supplements to the image, but it is the vivid central picture that drives the reflection. There is not a set order in which a response like this is read—the viewer's eye wanders around the page, taking in the whole, returning to different corners of the picture, adding up the elements that create the thought, finding different nuances and connections.

In a recent class on the structures of knowledge, which explores the history of current concepts of curriculum as well as what it means to be a "curriculum creator," Nathan broke down linear thinking barriers in his visual tour of TylerCo, Makers of Fine Curriculum Manufacturing Equipment (see Figure 11–7). As he sat at the dinner table one evening, Nathan created this flowchart in response to Tyler's classic 1947 text on learning objectives. In the drawings he blends his understanding of Tyler's beliefs about the need to create different kinds of learning objectives, the impact this has had on contemporary curriculum development, and the theoretical frameworks that are at odds with this view. In Stage 3, for example, one of the workers in the factory wears a "Freire Rules" T-shirt and gripes about the instrumentalist objectives. Humor—with an edge—abounds: the baker in Stage 2B says, "Each one o' these babies gets a content in the middle of some behaviors. Objectives sandwiches, we call 'em!" and a sign in the Stage 5 Evaluation room urges "Reuse/ Recycle: Remember . . . if it didn't meet your objectives, it may meet someone else's."

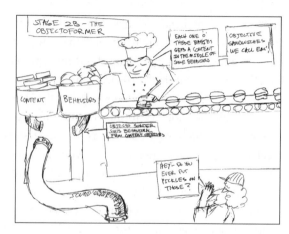

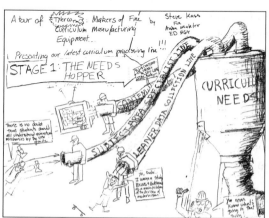

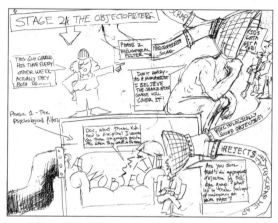

FIGURE 11–7

Introducing Visual Thinking to Adult Learners

Visual thinking challenges adults to experience things in a new way, enlarges their possibilities for understanding, gives them new tools for reflection, and expands their ideas of what it means to learn and teach. However, it can strike terror in the hearts of experienced learners who are quite comfortable, thank you, with the ways they have become accustomed to making meaning in classrooms. Though a few adults are delighted when they see me enter class armed with markers, crayons, and colored chalk, the majority react with nervousness or outright panic: Oh, no—I think she's gonna make us *draw*.

How can we help students take the initial plunge into visual thinking and learning? First and most important, by being a part of the process with them. When our students draw pictures of their "teaching brains," Andra and I do too, sharing our sketches and diagrams just as we share our response papers and excerpts from our journals. Though it's a risk to put out first-draft thinking in this way, it demonstrates that we're all in this together. A vital corollary is to

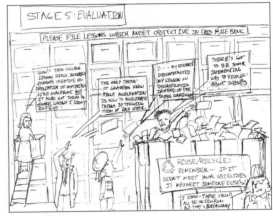

make the classroom safe enough for us to take these risks, to provide a net—a supportive learning environment—ready to catch us.

It also helps to encourage students to hold their standards in abeyance. Setting in-class time limits forces students to work quickly, to focus on the process rather than the product. Showing that even stick figures and simple shapes can symbolize sophisticated meaning often lessens the tension for students new to playing with images, who often lament, But I'm not a good enough artist.

Adults often need to learn to incorporate a change of pace into their quest for knowledge, to lighten up a little and allow playfulness to creep in. This can be a challenge—and a risk. In teaching this way we risk being perceived as less academic, less rigorous, than instructors who take a more traditional approach. Though this possibility always nags at the back of my mind and is occasionally reinforced by comments in journals or at evaluation conferences, it is strongly countered by my vision of what is possible for the adults I work with—and for the thousands of students they will teach and influence throughout their professional careers. Even the adults who don't choose to explore visual solutions beyond the whole-class experiments have a heightened awareness of the tool it can be for others around them and for their own students.

Naomi, a middle school teacher, confided that she was amazed to hear one of her group members comment that creating the *Beloved* collages had been the most powerful learning experience of the summer. "I learned from the group drawings and thought about the novel in different ways," Naomi told me, "but it wasn't the really strong experience that it was for many of the others in the class. Writing is really comfortable for me—a natural way to explore and make sense of what I read. Though I probably won't choose to draw in response to reading, I have a better understanding of ways it might be helpful for some of my own students. To tell you the truth, it makes me empathize with students who don't love to write, as I do. It helps to put myself more in their position trying something different like drawing, seeing what it might do for me."

Naomi touches on another important reason for bringing art into teacher education: educators need to be genuine practitioners of outlets they want children to be able to explore. If teachers and parents feel intimidated by and remote from art, they are going to pass those feelings on to the children in their lives.

Maxine Greene writes eloquently about how important it is to awaken children to the arts as a way of understanding. "To feel oneself en route, to feel oneself in a place where there are always possibilities of clearings, of new openings: this is what we hope to communicate to the young, if we want to awaken them to their lived situations, enable them to make sense, to name their worlds" (1991, p. 37). We can best clear those paths if we go down them with the children, expanding the notion of what literacy can be for all of us, writers and artists, adults and children.

References

Cameron, J. 1992. *The Artist's Way: A Spiritual Path to Higher Creativity.* New York: Jeremy P. Tarcher/Putnam Books.

Greene, M. 1991. "Texts and Margins." *Harvard Educational Review* 61(1):27–39.

Lionni, L. 1984. "Before Images." *The Horn Book* 60(6):727–34.

Morrison, T. 1987. *Beloved.* New York: Alfred Knopf.

Tyler, R. 1947. *Basic Principles of Curriculum and Instruction.* Chicago: University of Chicago Press.

12

Background, Foreground: From Experience to Classroom Practice

Karen Ernst

The classroom bulletin board is filled with paintings, drawings, and collages. Chatter and laughter rise from a table of painters. Some people sit alone; some work with a friend. Classical music lightens the warm air. Peter and Cathy sit drawing in the school yard, their sketch boards propped on their laps. Mary Ellen colors carefully inside the lines of the cow she has copied from a picture book. Jeanne's left hand is suspended in air as she captures it in a contour drawing. Lesley sits alone at a desk, adding touches to the field of poppies she has been working on the entire week. Dawn uses oil pastels for her version of a Kandinsky, while Liz mixes paint colors for her copy of a seascape by Winslow Homer.

Other people are writing in their journals. Mary Sue, responding to Lesley's poppies in progress, imagines, "As I sit on my front porch and look out into the field of poppies, I feel a calmness come over me. It's early morning and the sun is continuing to rise. The quiet and stillness of the meadow are relaxing."

Liz's entry focuses on her process: "It's amazing the colors you can create. Today I also love the product even though I had just as much fun with the whole experience. I'm writing like a second grader! Maybe that's how I feel. That is the most important thing that this week has done for me. It has let me see the world like a child again; to look at things in a new way. To study them, to notice things, to think, reflect, and share."

Dana really likes her oil pastel and watercolor of ducks, copied from a picture book: "I have not done any personal artwork for many years. I am surprised that my work is very similar to what I did twenty years ago. It makes me wonder if I am just picking up where I left off."

Experience Before Practice

For one week in the last days of summer, when most teachers are thinking about setting up their classroom and worrying about meeting new students, a

mary jane, pam, robin
mary ... [illegible], lisa, [illegible], jane, kathy

group of teachers at Kings Highway Elementary School returned to the world of childhood to learn about the role of art as a means of expression, to experience the parallel processes of art and writing, and to raise questions about how they would and could connect art and writing in their elementary classrooms.

This seminar was their first step toward infusing art into their writers workshops in their K–4 classrooms. The teachers were working with me, the school's art specialist, to learn how the visual arts can make important contributions to the writers workshop and across the curriculum.

The subject of our inquiry was, What happens when art becomes part of the writers workshop? Our goal was for each teacher to incorporate art into the curriculum based on individual style as well as on grade level appropriateness. The teachers kept research journals that focused on their own learning and observations. Later each teacher collected examples of student work to show how what they learned emerged in their own classroom.

Background: Teachers in the Studio

Each day of the summer workshop included a presentation by a teacher who had participated in an earlier pilot version. These presentations were the foundation for important classroom routines. For example, Mary Sue gave tips on managing portfolios. Peter talked about how he uses sketch journals with his fourth graders (see Chapter 9 in this book). These practical models encouraged all participants to make both of these techniques part of their curriculum.

Several times throughout the day teachers painted, sketched, and wrote, shared their pictures and writing, and raised questions about classroom implementation. The sense of community was strengthened by their willingness to take risks, the stories they shared about their experiences, and my perspective as an elementary art teacher who had previously taught middle school English for twenty years.

The model for this artists/writers summer workshop was the workshop I use in my own art classroom. We began with a rehearsal—reading a picture book, looking at the work of an artist or of a colleague—to help us focus on ideas for our own work. I demonstrated how to use materials available in the room—acrylic paints, watercolors, markers, crayons, oil pastels, and drawing pens—and then each person chose a topic and a medium and went to work. Not only were the structure and routine similar to those in my student workshops, so were the process and results. The participants' work influenced how they looked at their surroundings and how they valued choice, risk taking, sharing, and community. They wrote about the exciting process of making pictures; they were surprised when they wrote in a voice unlike one they had heard before; and in responding to one another's pictures and feelings, they revealed their own imagination.

At first Jeanne was reluctant to attempt a picture. She felt that she had no ideas, that she couldn't do this, and she didn't want to take the risk. By the end of the week she was bemoaning, "I'll never have enough time to finish everything I want to try!" Her first picture, a delicate, wispy watercolor flower, prompted her to risk drawing her hand in contour. Eventually she painted more abstract works and wrote poetry. She observed, " I noticed how much I enjoyed having the command and ownership over what I created this week. I could ask for help and suggestions when I needed or wanted them. I felt pressure free, and I felt good about what I was doing." Allowed to say I can instead of I can't, she asked questions that propelled her work in the classroom as she made choices across the curriculum. "If I feel so strongly about being in charge of my own learning, and I have kids now in charge of their own artwork and writing, how can I translate this into other curricular areas?"

Kristi wrote about her own collage, "I can see now why artists keep going back and repainting the same scene. Even now I'm imagining how I could bring about the same scene in a different medium. Do kids often keep drawing the same types of pictures because they too are looking for more satisfying ways of catching the mood or feel of the picture?" Kristi's experience meant that she returned to her classroom with more understanding of why her students draw and write in certain ways.

Just like the students in our classrooms, the teachers in this workshop found their own process of discovery exciting, something to write about. Peter described his frustration with drawing in contour; Liz described her process of painting, the feeling of being " carried away with making the waves and playing with colors. That led into the sky, where I mixed paint in streaks. I don't even know if I like what I made, but I liked how I felt when I was making it. It felt daring and creative." Liz realized that the process can be as exciting as the product, that there is a freeing sense of discovery when risk taking is valued.

Some mornings we sat in silence and wrote responses to yesterday's pictures, which were pinned to the bulletin board. I asked my colleagues to "read" the pictures—to notice where their eyes stopped, consider why they were interested in a certain picture, tell the story captured in the image, discuss the technique being used. This not only helped us learn how to look and respond but also led to a deeper sense of community, to an awareness of the uniqueness of each person's view—the maker's and the responder's.

Peter's rumination about Jane's whimsical painting—a house, a rabbit leaping over its roof top, and the moon tilted in the sky overhead—helped him deal with his impending move to a new house. Liz, reluctant to speak in large groups, passed her journal around the circle. Expressing herself primarily through words and pictures on paper, she was a reminder that we need to respect the variety of learning styles in our classroom, to open the door to many ways of expression.

Looking at one another's work, responding to it, making pictures, taking risks, and sharing brought us together, helped us respect our own process of learning and that of others. It demonstrated what we wanted our future classrooms to hold—a community of learners in which each person could participate, to which each person could contribute.

For Dawn the sense of community and the new connection she had with her colleagues were more important than her two Kandinsky-inspired pictures: "I am proud of the artwork but even prouder of the feeling about doing artwork within this group of people." She noted how the feelings of anxiety, apprehension, and fear and the hints of anger changed as the week progressed. People overcame self-consciousness, complimented each other, said what they saw, laughed, were immersed in a process together. She wrote about her experiences with people, not just her choices in media: being impressed that Liz "felt daring," getting to know Jeanne through her writing and pictures.

On the last day the walls displayed pictures in a variety of styles and the echoes of the accompanying writing reverberated in the room. Our colleagues appeared unique. Peter reflected on the week-long experience this way: "For me, to watch people growing, changing, emerging as the week progressed readily reinforced the power of this idea. All the teachers seemed to come into focus for me as individuals with distinct styles, gifts, backgrounds, tendencies, awarenesses, and needs. I think that our doing art, which on the first day seemed to separate us into the talented and the artistically challenged, also blended us together. We wrote, we talked, we observed, and we thought, and as we did, the differences in style, vision, and technique became less differences in quality than differences in personality—differences among individuals, among humans. Looking at the pictures is inspiring to me now—not just because they look beautiful, but because of the faces and words I see floating in the background, like a spirit."

Foreground: Teachers in the Classroom

The collaboration that began in the summer continued throughout the year; the teachers had a common language and foundation for further learning. I talked with them about the developments in their classroom. They kept sketch journals and collected student work that reflected the ways their classroom was changing. We discussed questions, findings, and new insights in biweekly meetings.

Teachers began staying in the art room with their class, observing their students and working on their own pictures and writing. They became models for their students' learning. The teachers' pictures displayed on the bulletin board often inspired student work. Dana's ducks became a challenge for a second grader; Liz's boat—the one that made her feel "daring"—launched numerous student versions. A first grader spent weeks copying a picture Hallie had done in the summer workshop. The two pictures were displayed side by side in the townwide art show, demonstrating how our learning community was widening.

The teachers in two adjoining fourth-grade classes combined their artists/writers workshops—shared minilessons, with a "quiet room" and a "conferring room." Dawn opened her classroom to parents who wanted to learn more about the curriculum. The mother of one student came to artists/writers workshop once a week, writing, making pictures, submitting her work for class response, another learner in this ever-wider community of learners. The notion of learning through experience and observation prompted a new sense of what a "writers community" is; teachers were better able to break the barriers of isolation they often experience in education.

Fourth graders conducted an "artists share" in a second-grade class; a first grader shared her work in a third-grade class. The common language and understanding between teachers made it possible for "buddy" classes to have a joint artists/writers workshop in which writing and art were shared across the two grades. Students recognized experts and learned from each other regardless of age.

First graders took their sketch journals on a field trip to a farm where they drew and wrote about the cows, the chickens, the barn. Second graders sat on the front lawn of the school and captured the daffodils in pencil sketches and in words. Classes finished in the artists workshop and carried their notebooks to the classroom, where their teacher provided time for silent writing about what they did in art. Reading in a second-grade classroom had a new impetus and meaning as the teacher directed the students to focus on the pictures and the language. Teachers and students saw a wider need for art and writing; the sketch journals provided a way to reach across the curriculum. Students began to read through the lenses of artists and writers, looking for new ways to paint with words or read with pictures.

Rikki sat in the artist/author chair in her first-grade classroom, reading the words she'd clipped to the back of her picture, which she had made first. Mary Ellen asked the class to listen for pictures they saw in their imagination as Rikki read. In another classroom classical music played softly as the second graders leaned into their writing. Dawn had initiated the twenty-minute silent writing period by reading a piece a student had written the day before. Darcy and her third-grade students were hard at work in their artists/writers workshop. She divided her attention between her own watercolor painting and the works her students were writing, creating, and discussing. She was very aware that modeling herself as a learner was a key to good teaching. In a fourth-grade classroom, Peter led a minilesson using pages from his sketch journal to show his students how drawing and writing would help them look at their surroundings, reflect on their thinking, and experience being observers, which would in turn make them better writers. His students carried their journals from artists workshop into their classroom so they could use them to draw, write, and think about their learning in reading, science, social studies, and of course writing. At an after-school meeting a kindergarten teacher explained how she had come to respect the meaning and power of the pictures that her young authors produced. Her focus in writers workshop had changed: she no longer forced her students to write stories but let them use pictures as a springboard for writing.

A Different Perspective on Teaching and Learning

At Kings Highway the writers workshop is now called the artists/writers workshop. We have turned away from the ideas about art we learned in school and embraced what kindergartners know naturally: a picture is a form of expression, holds meaning, and is a story, a poem, a reflection of thinking.

The teachers' experiences as artists and learners in the summer seminar let them "relive a few moments of childhood," as Liz wrote in her journal. "It has helped me get in touch with the frightened feelings I experienced—the insecurities. I think I can now be more sensitive to the kids in my class who all come with their own doubts. I want to make my classroom a safer place next year, a place to take risks, to express thoughts, to share, to think, to learn, and to feel. My priority has to be our learning, not my teaching."

Many of these teachers had had their picture making halted many years ago by someone who said, You are not an artist, or, You did not draw that in the right way. Perhaps after spending some time trying to stay inside the lines or making something perfect, they gave up. Now they were getting another chance. Together they took risks, laughed with one another, and responded to one another's ideas. They watched their students create portfolios of artwork and built their own art portfolios. They came to a new understanding of the need for multiple forms of expression, for turning mistakes into successes. They discovered new voices and experienced the delight of creation, a delight that freed them from the worries of going outside the boundaries of a line. They learned that experience is the important background for their work in the classroom.

Mary Ellen wrote about her first-grade class, "The artists/writers workshop in my classroom has changed my writing program in many ways. In the beginning of the year, one of the biggest differences for me as a teacher was allowing the students' pictures to take on a new significance—giving the artwork power as a valued expression of the students' thoughts. In previous years I felt a great deal of pressure to have the children start cranking out pieces of writing to be made into published books." This new value on pictures has expanded our publishing possibilities. Many teachers encourage students to publish a finished picture with or without accompanying text or to exhibit it in classroom galleries or other school locations.

Kristi found that picture making in the writers workshop gave her children access to more tools for expression. She increased her own knowledge about drawing by taking a class and using that knowledge to help her students connect drawing with observing and writing. Elizabeth noted that picture making has made students more invested in their workshop time and stimulated a wider range of writing—descriptions, reflections, explanations, poems, and stories. For students who have difficulty in writing, picture making becomes the essential springboard. There is more writing across the curriculum, and for both students and teachers, writing in the artists/writers workshop seems more natural, less stressful and forced.

Darcy concentrated on helping her third graders understand the connection between picture making and revision. She discovered that once a picture was revised, her students naturally revised their writing about the picture as well. Revision is literally reseeing; a picture makes this difficult skill concrete. A student in Darcy's class said, "If you couldn't do art, you couldn't see your thoughts."

Our teachers know that a picture can be the bridge to writing. By sharing their pictures, their writing, and their thinking, students increase their verbal and listening skills. The artists/writers workshop lasts longer and students are able to undertake sustained silent writing for longer periods. Teachers take their classes to area art museums where students sketch and respond to works of art in their sketch journals. Picture making embraces the reluctant writer and makes a place for him or her as a respected member of the classroom community. Children broaden their art to go with their writing and vice versa. The enthusiasm for artists/writers workshop is high and productivity has increased. The partnership of pictures and writing in the artists/writers workshops at Kings Highway has enhanced writing and thinking, broadened ways of publishing and revising, and given both students and teachers new tools for teaching and learning.

In our project to discover the connections between art and writing, learning theory worked hand in hand with a teacher's own experience. These teachers were not carrying out prescribed methodologies but were reformulating theory in light of their own experience and using what they learned to strengthen their classroom and the school. They discovered that reading, writing, and picture making are important preparations for teaching.

Liz shared an essay she wrote about her professional and personal growth:

lesley painting her poppies.

I've noticed many dramatic changes in myself as a learner/teacher that I believe have occurred as a result of my participation in this project. I am still the same person, but I've discovered a part of myself that I never before believed existed . . . an artist!

I guess I am really reliving a certain aspect of childhood. I'm really learning to really look at things closely and examine details. Everything I see that interests me, I want to draw. My journal is my partner. I use it to take notes on what my students say and do. I sketch, take notes, and reflect on my teaching.

What a valuable experience to literally take the child's point of view. I have found that I'm able to be much more sensitive to the students' insecurities and questions. I write and draw with my class constantly to model myself as a learner, artist, writer, and thinker. I watch the kids differently. I approach the whole process differently. I learn so much about my students by sketching them and writing about them. I value their picture making as a means of self-expression. Art and writing have become partners in our classroom.

13

Drawing My Selves Together:
An Editor's Notebook

Toby Gordon

To be a good editor, you need to get out of the way. You listen for other people's ideas, draw them out, reveal their potential. Authors shine, you stay in the background.

And in the process, editors often edit themselves. While we encourage others to find their voices, we're in danger of losing our own. But occasionally, if we're lucky, a book we're editing will trigger a far-off memory. We then reclaim a part of ourselves through the words of others.

Reading the manuscript of Karen Ernst's *Picturing Learning* (1994), I was struck by the similarities—and painful differences—of our early experiences. She colored so hard in kindergarten she could "feel the coloring bump rise on my middle finger"; while the other students put away their materials, her teacher allowed her to finish her drawing. "It was then I knew I wanted to be an artist."

I too colored fiercely in kindergarten. I too had a hard callous on my right-hand middle finger—the finger I gripped the crayons with as I drew my way through Mrs. Ferguson's tough teaching.

Every day we got to choose one activity for our twenty minutes of free time. There were a lot of materials from which to choose, but every day I got out the crayons and the clean white paper. For me, there was no choice—coloring was what I *had* to do. For a short time I lost myself through shapes and color and escaped the criticism of this hard woman.

And then Mrs. Ferguson gave me the blow—"No, not today, Toby. You can do *anything* but color."

I flinched, blushed madly, looked around for another choice and found Tinkertoys. I didn't know what to do with them. I stuck two wooden disks at the ends of a stick and pretended they were barbells. I lifted the stick as if it were heavy and grunted. I did nothing. I was pathetic.

Twenty minutes later, I heard Mrs. Ferguson's voice: "Everyone come to the rug now to hear a story. And while we sit here, Toby will remain at her desk, playing with the Tinkertoys. She doesn't know how to play with them yet."

Left alone at the wooden table, playing with the Tinkertoys, I knew I would never forgive my kindergarten teacher. Nor would I ever choose crayons again as a way of creating my own sense of comfort.

My fate was sealed. Coloring was out for me. It was frivolous, wasteful, not the serious stuff of school or my life. Even Tinkertoys were more important. So I made my way—choosing words as my passport—becoming the good student who wrote her book reports on time in elementary school, her five-paragraph themes neatly in high school, and her deconstructions of the deconstructivists in graduate school.

But all along, the callous on my middle finger remained hard—secretly I doodled on napkins, on backs of envelopes, on last week's shopping list. I coveted pens and markers and mechanical pencils were best of all. In my next life, I would own a stationery store.

And then my secret life slowly came to the surface. Editing *Picturing Learning*—and reading how Karen's kindergarten teacher allowed her to finish her drawing—I started to remember who I once had been. The girl who couldn't stop drawing—until Mrs. Ferguson stopped me dead in my tracks.

"But I'm an editor," I told Karen as she nudged me to start drawing again. "I edit books. I do words, not pictures. It would be too embarrassing to see how bad my drawings were."

But I couldn't resist her nudges. We would meet at conferences around the country, and everywhere we went I would watch her make sense of the world through writing and pictures in her artist's notebook. She never stopped. There was no self-consciousness on her part. Her notebook was a critical part of who she was.

And as I watched her, my own life began to change—first at work and then outside the office. Mrs. Ferguson's reign had ended. I came back to who I had been before I closed up.

Karen got me going, but where was I headed? My work life used to be contained within stenographer pads—those small, lined pads, spiral bound at the top. I would fill them with cramped lists of things to do. I went through them quickly, pinning back the used pages with a black binder clip. They were efficient and neat. Period. They contained nothing of me—only lists of people to call, letters to write, contracts to arrange. There was no room to spread out, loosen up, think. And at the time, I didn't know that's what I was after.

Then I bought an eight-and-a-half-by-eleven-inch, blank-paged sketch pad, and I felt my former self begin to crack open. I still create unending lists—I

Shelley Harwayne.

Some of the best writing during
the day was during science.

Parents' response: "I could do th

ⓧ Children's anthology —
"You mean that's writing?"

Ann Turner, Street Talk.

Only the Moon + Me, (OP)
Richard Margolis

"Making sense of their 3 minutes
here on earth."

Beautiful thought
squeezed into this
mucky muck mess.

We got these kids wide awake —
we got them looking at the world.

Who are the B

Here's to all the fathers who
share peaches w/ their children

The shape, the architecture, of a
picture book is manageable —
                         picture books

Images of grandmother/building up →
...I could do that! It's not so
                              complicated
Joanne Ryder — My Father's Hands

Life in the underground —

"You just give it away. This stuff
                    is so good."

FIGURE 13-1

don't know an editor who doesn't. (How else does one keep track of projects in development, manuscripts to appear, book costings, budgets, artwork, permissions, conferences to attend, people to visit?) The innumerable details of an editor's life are overwhelming—by writing them down, we save, as one of my colleagues calls it, "our precious mental space" for other, more important, matters.

So, in this way the "before" stenographer-pad lists look like the "after" sketchbook lists. But with a slight twist. Before there were only lists—tight little words filling up the pages. No embellishments. No white space. Just boring lists.

But now, when I want it, I have room to roam. On the phone, in meetings, at conferences, I decorate, doodle, make the pages visually appealing. While talking with authors and colleagues, I let my pen go. My hand stays busy, and my listening becomes more active and acute. Their words, and my thinking about their words, fill up the pages. Faces, figures, and designs float in the margins. And later my words and images—as inaccurate as they may be—will bring me right back to the precise moment of a long-ago meeting, conversation, or conference. The tone of the moment lingers in the white space. I can't lose it now. And from there I can turn it around, play with it, hold it; I can recapture old feeling states and generate new ideas.

Keeping Moments Alive

Looking at my sketch of Shelley Harwayne while she presented at a recent University of New Hampshire conference (Figure 13–1), I remember her wit and wisdom. I remember her fast talk, the books she recommended, the love she has for her students and her work. I caught her words—"We've got these kids wide awake, we've got them looking at the world"; "Here's to all the fathers who share peaches with their children"; "The shape, the architecture of a picture book is manageable." They're all reminders to me of why she *must* write about the Manhattan New School, of which she is the principal.

On another page I see Lad Tobin giving a talk at NCTE on better ways to read student papers (Figure 13–2). I'm impressed with the second half of the talk; he's warmed up, he's cooking. The first half though should go—he needs to cut to the chase, skip the theory, and tell his audience what happens in his classroom between him, his students, and the written page. I listen, keep track of his argument, mentally edit an unwritten paper. We talk afterwards (not an unusual thing, since he's my husband), and I show him my notes. He agrees with my suggestions.

Next to the drawing of him I read, "a massive horde of mosquitoes takes off

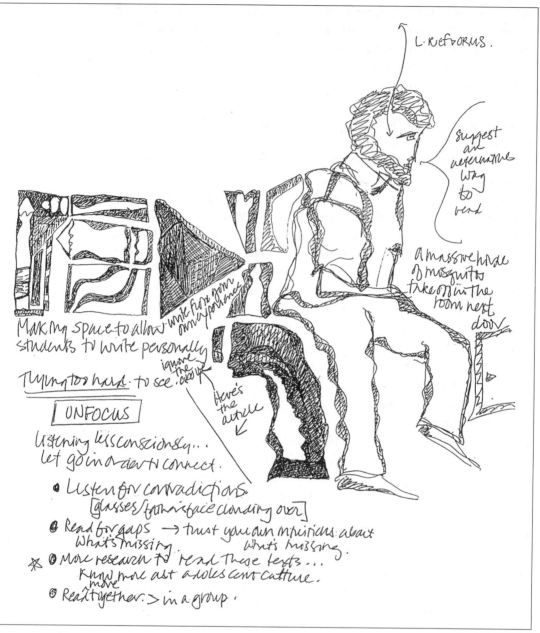

FIGURE 13–2

in the room next door." The audience on the other side of the screen broke into small group discussions; they completely drowned him out for a minute. Did he hear it? No. I'm struck by what happens, or doesn't happen, to our senses when we're immersed in the "flow" of the moment. The memory may not be important, but it makes up a fragment of a moment of his life and mine.

So, in a loose, haphazard, unconscious kind of way, I make the notebooks mine. In the end, I craft the notebooks—and they become a reflection of what I did, what I need to do, think, imagine, and where I want to go. My notebooks have turned from being a catalog of tasks to be completed to an illustrated chronicle of my life as an editor. Are they beautiful? No. Am I embarrassed by my drawings? No. Do they matter? You bet.

Trying on Ideas

How else do I use my notebook? I try out different cover designs:

I work out a math problem that appears in a manuscript I'm considering:

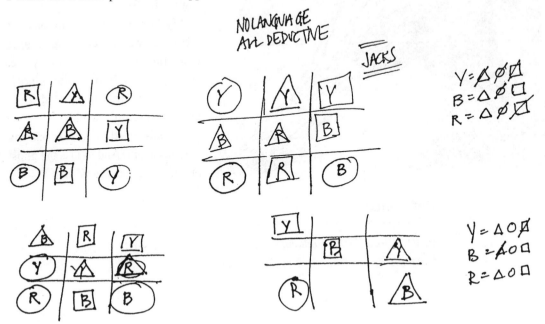

I list all of the editors' forthcoming titles to get a sense of next year's list.

My notebook provides me with space to test ideas, try out solutions, and keep track of my thinking. Like the stenographer's pad, it is still very functional—but again with a difference. There are no black lines to hem me in or hold me back. Anything can happen now. It's what I make of it.

Life Outside the Office Walls

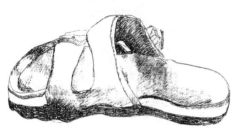

And once my notebooks started loosening me up *inside* the office, I started loosening up *outside* the office. Drawing became an everyday, natural activity for me again, not something reserved for the backs of envelopes. "Doing words," I realized, was only one side of myself. I started taking weekly art lessons and caught glimpses of potential.

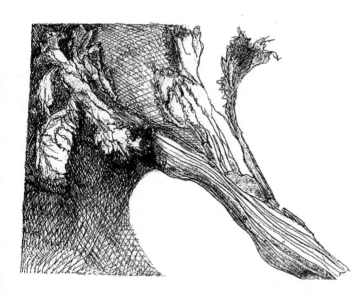

I then started blending my "outside world" attempts with my editor's notebook. Flying across the country to a conference in California, I put aside the manuscript I was reading and let my pencil go (see Figure 13–3).

My former, rigid notions of where drawings belong no longer hold true. The more I draw, write, and try poetry in my editor's notebook, the more I blur the distinctions between my worlds.

It feels good to break out my crayons again. And to kiss the ghost of Mrs. Ferguson good-bye.

References

Ernst, Karen. 1994. *Picturing Learning: Artists and Writers in the Classroom.* Portsmouth, NH: Heinemann

CAPE COD WINTER WINDOWS
12·1·94.

FLYING OVER NYC TO SF

A SHARPENED PENCIL ALWAYS MAKES ME DRAW.

Carl Brenders's Lord of the Marshes, 1988

12·1·94

FIGURE 13-3

Contributors

Susan Benedict is currently a second-grade teacher at the Park School in Brooklandville, Maryland. Her essay in this volume chronicles her work with fifth and sixth graders at the Center for Teaching and Learning in Edgecomb, Maine.

Jean Anne Clyde is an associate professor of literacy at the University of Louisville in Kentucky. She enjoys exploring her interests—multiple ways of knowing, inquiry-based learning, and early literacy—with kids and teachers in area schools.

Irene C. Fountas is a professor of education at Lesley College in Cambridge, Massachusetts. She has worked as a classroom teacher and language arts specialist in public schools for more than twenty years.

Toby Gordon is the education publisher at Heinemann, in Portsmouth, New Hampshire.

Janet L. Olson is chair of the art education department at Boston University School for the Arts. She is also the author of *Envisioning Writing: Toward an Integration of Drawing and Writing* (Heinemann, 1992).

Jill Ostrow currently teaches a multiage class of first through third graders in the West Linn/Wilsonville School District in Oregon. She is the author of *A Room with a Different View* (Stenhouse, 1995).

Brenda Power is an associate professor of literacy at the University of Maine, where she teaches courses in language, literacy, and research. She edits *Teacher Research: The Journal of Classroom Inquiry.*

Mary Stein is with the department of science education at Wayne State University in Detroit, Michigan. She taught high school science in western New York State and was a recipient of the National Science Teachers' Association Science Teaching Achievement Recognition (STAR) Award.

Peter Thacker is a longtime high school reading specialist and English teacher in Portland, Oregon. He is committed to renewing himself through creative endeavors.

Peter von Euler has taught fourth grade in Westport, Connecticut, for ten years, the last six at Kings Highway School.

Nancy Winterbourne has taught first and second grade in Molalla, Oregon, for twenty years.